MENTORING

THE

NEW EXECUTIVE

"Old Guard" Meets
"New Attitude"

Kevin Michael Struck

Library of Congress Cataloging-in-Publication Data

Struck, Kevin Michael, 1962-
  Mentoring the new executive : "old guard" meets "new attitude" /
Kevin Michael Struck.
    p. cm.
  ISBN 1-932133-19-4 (pbk. : alk. paper)
  1. Executives—Training of. 2. Business ethics. 3. Mentoring in
business. I. Title.
  HD30.4 .S766 2003
  658.4'07124--dc21

                          2002151184

Published by The Writers' Collective in 2003.
A previous version of Chapter 15 appeared in the
Feb.- Mar., 2002 issue of *Communication World*.

Cover and interior design by
Mary Struck © 2003, Terra Media, L.L.C.

Original stock photographs featured on cover by Comstock.com
and AbleStock.com™

Retro Clipart by permission from niftykeen.com, clipmart.com,
loti.com and Corel.

Characters featured in this book are fictional and not
representative of cover models.

CONTENTS

ACKNOWLEDGMENTS

This book probably first took root in my mind when I sat daydreaming one day in yet another tedious conference workshop. If that long since forgotten speaker had been even the least bit interesting, I might never have begun the train of thought that led to this book. To him I am grateful.

More seriously, I'd like to thank Gloria Gordon, chief editor at *Communication World*, for publishing a version of what has since become Chapter 15 of this book. It was the very first chapter I wrote, and its success—along with a suggestion from my wife, Mary—ultimately led to all of the subsequent chapters.

Mary was an indispensable part of this book's creation, making innumerable valuable suggestions, and, most importantly, designing the cover.

I am also grateful to Jean Cooksey, an editor I first met while writing for OnWord Press. This book would be sorely lacking without her substantial contributions as editor.

Finally, many thanks to the resourceful Lisa Grant and her staff at The Writers' Collective for patiently and cheerfully coordinating the publishing end of it all.

PREFACE

With almost daily reports of scandal and intrigue surrounding executives at major corporations, the time appears ripe for younger managers to step forward with fresh alternatives for how business is conducted. The ascending generation has already made a *cultural* impact on the business world by relaxing dress codes, shortening meetings, and integrating technology.

But, what about *ethics?* How much of an impact will the new generation have on personal conduct, employee relations, financial accountability, and consumer welfare? Or, will it be "business as usual" as too many new executives eventually fall prey to the ethics-shredding allure of power, greed, and self-importance?

These are questions this book, of course, cannot answer. Only the individuals rising to power in the next few years can determine the outcome. From now until then, there will be plenty of sober examinations of the failings of the "old guard," along with calls-to-action and well-reasoned arguments exhorting the next generation of executives to "raise the bar" and "clean things up." It is unlikely, however, that much of the intended audience will read such "lectures."

With this in mind, I set out to write a book that would accomplish the same purpose, but in a more entertaining style and format. By portraying the worst of the "old guard," I hoped to paint an embarrassing picture of what awaits the next generation of leaders if they follow the path of least resistance. Call it aversion therapy. For added kicks, I've tossed in a representative of the next generation or "new attitude."

Representing the old guard, retired CEO Henry Ablebright's zeal for mentoring new executives has remained unhampered by the recent corporate accounting scandals and indictments of several high-profile executives. Blinded by his own beaming pride, he has no idea what kind of a mentor he really is.

Nicholas Marten, representing the new attitude, turns out to be less ready and willing to accept the instructions offered him than his mentor expects. Mr. Marten, of course, is not perfect—nevertheless, he is full of potential.

In their book *Generations at Work,* authors Ron Zemke, Claire Raines, and Bob Filipczak state: "Walk through the . . . corridors of America's businesses, and what do you hear? *Not* the sounds of harmony. Instead, you'll probably hear the grumbles of irritation as people with wholly different ways of working, talking, and thinking have been tossed together side by side, cubicle by cubicle. It's the teeth-gritting sound of generations in collision." The severity of the collision remains to be seen.

Now, I had best get out of the way: My creations are clambering to introduce themselves.

– **Kevin Michael Struck**

INTRODUCTION

HENRY ABLEBRIGHT: *Be Like Me*

I don't generally need an introduction, but for the few who don't know me, I'm Henry Ablebright, recently retired President and CEO of Ablebright Manufacturing Corporation. Friends and long-time associates call me "Hub." You'll get nothing but practical advice from me—no bug-eyed academic theories, no trite maxims from an "expert" who couldn't run a lemonade stand, and no pointless rambling from a moth-balled manager who only runs a business in his memory.

You can be just like me someday if you work at it. With a little persistence, you can think like me, talk like me, dress like me, and act like me. Don't think you can do it? Ah, you're not giving yourself enough credit. You'd be surprised what you're capable of. Just follow me.

One Saturday morning, I drove through the office parking lot at my company to see who had worked through the night—as usual, there were precious few. Mixed feelings of pride and concern came over me. I have spent a productive and satisfying life helping to lead several of the post-World War II corporations that are the backbone of the quality of life that millions of consumers now enjoy.

As I got back on the freeway, however, I pondered the inevitability that the mantle of leadership will soon be handed to the next generation of managers. They must ensure that products and services remain plentiful. Many observers claim the newcomers are unprepared for such a challenge—witness the dot-com debacle—and that productivity is due for a decline. It is not by accident that the youngest generations have been named after letters at the *bottom* of the alphabet.

This is an awfully sobering assessment, but I have faith in you. Or, rather, faith in my ability as a mentor. I take this calling very seriously. Certainly you have heard, "Those who can, do. Those who cannot, teach." This can be taken one pitiful step further: "Those who are not sure whether they can or cannot, assist." It is my job to equip you to "do."

Hence my contributions to this book, written with the knowledge that the early years of a future executive's career are the most formative and therefore paramount. Fortunately, mentors like me have a broader window of opportunity. The generation currently entering management has not matured as quickly as previous ones. My eldest brother was leading squadrons onto limb-strewn South Pacific beachheads at the age of 18; most young folks today risk only blisters as they play the latest video games.

In contributing to this book I also had in mind the millions of young, disenfranchised entrepreneurs eking out a paltry existence today in lonely isolation from the corporate mainland. Sooner or later, they will recover from their presumptuousness, and when they do, they will need help regaining their land legs in the mainstream business world.

I will not kid anyone. Filling the shoes of the current and retired generations of executives will take a strong focus. Nevertheless, the upcoming generation must not faint at the prospect. You must instead heed our words and strive to imitate our examples, knowing that if you can become even *half* of the executives we were, civilization will hobble forward.

NICHOLAS MARTEN: *Our Turn*

My name is Nicholas Marten. I used to be a junior-level manager at Ablebright Manufacturing. Currently, I run my own recording studio where I go by the name of "Nick Tragic."

Where do I start after Hub's intro? First of all, I know it's hard to imagine, but every company in the country will one day be run by someone of my generation. I'm betting the Fortune 500 will never be the same. Who knows, we might finally scrap English measurements.

Hub and his cronies seem to think we newcomers need all of this "mentoring" or we're doomed. I hate to appear ungrateful, but does anybody really know what the hell they're doing? Just hand over the flashlight and we'll find our own way in the dark.

H: *The Fall*

The sentences that follow on the next few pages were not easy for me to write. Yet, I have persevered with the hope that the words will serve as a solemn warning to young professionals. You will be tempted by today's twisted "popular culture" to cast aside the shining future your elders have made possible for you. Sadly, there are some among you who will laugh off my warning as so much bluster from an aging relic. Such individuals are already teetering perilously close to destruction.

It is with profound regret that I think of the downward spiral of an individual who was becoming like a son to me. Nicholas once had so much potential—an MBA, a successful internship at a Fortune 500 company, and an attitude shinier than his well-polished wingtips. He admired all of the top CEOs (had even met Jack Welch), boasted about his diversified portfolio, and recently purchased his first Brooks Brothers suit. I even offered to lease Nicholas one of my Lincoln Town Cars, and I had included him in my entourage to Saratoga for the spring racing season.

Then, something went horribly wrong: This bright prodigy went over to your generation's dark side. His last visit to my office was as painful as it was tragic. Looking back, I should have seen it coming. There *were* signs.

Nicholas started coming in a tad late in the morning, looking like he'd been up all night. When I pressed him on it, he remained vague, mumbling something about some friends and a club. I knew full well that he wasn't talking about the country club.

"We had a short meeting with Bentley's exporter this morning," I'd say, or something similar.

"Whatever. . . ."

Then he'd shuffle—not stride—out of my office. I'd walk by later and see him sitting with three crumpled cans of Mountain Dew strewn across his desk. He'd have his tie pulled down and his hair, which he had at least attempted to comb back earlier, would be hanging in front of his rapidly shifting eyes.

After a few weeks of this erratic behavior, he shocked me by asking for a laptop computer with a wireless Internet connection and an MP3 player.

"A what?" I exclaimed. "What do you need all that for?"

"Everyone my age has one. Besides, it'll make me more efficient and stuff."

Like a father desperate to hang onto his wayward son, I relented, in the hope, I suppose, that my financial support would bring him back under my influence. For a short time it worked. I had my collar-starched Nicholas back again. Yet, there was something different about him. No longer did the corporate image come naturally. His mannerisms appeared strained, as though beneath the surface a Jekyll-and-Hyde battle raged within. Once, in the limo on the way to our hangar, I caught him looking longingly out the window at a group of ragtag young ne'er-do-wells loitering like geese in a park. I was losing him.

The day of reckoning came one sunny morning when we should have been happy celebrating a two-for-one stock split. Nicholas had been off on a long weekend and was later than usual.

"Any messages from him?" I asked Liza, his secretary.

"No, nothing, Mr. Ablebright."

Just then, he appeared in the doorway. The sight of him sucked the breath out of my lungs. The fluorescent lights overhead flickered. I tried to shield Liza from catching a glimpse, but I was too late. Her eyes grew large as pepperonis, then she put a hand on her forehead and promptly fainted.

"You've got a lot of nerve showing up here like that!" I barked, hoping to cow him into obedience. "Now go back home and get into your suit and tie. We've got a client coming in for lunch."

Nicholas was unfazed as he slouched against the doorpost. He had begun to grow sideburns and something on his chin. Beneath the brim of his tight stocking cap I spotted a ring in his ear. He wore a nondescript hooded sweatshirt, baggy shorts, and hippie sandals.

"I hate to bail on you, but I'm here to give my notice," Nicholas said matter-of-factly.

"Oh, I see. And when is your last day?"

"Actually, I was kind of thinking it would be last Thursday."

My first instinct was outrage, but after quickly thinking it over, I was actually relieved. The sooner I could get him out of the building, the better. He would be a terrible influence on the other young professionals.

"Does Melanie approve of this?" I asked. Nicholas' girlfriend was a graduate student who had a bright future (and nice legs).

"Melanie's cool with it. She's into her thing, and I'm into mine. We respect each other."

Since when was respect the most important thing between a man and a girl? The poor kid's compass was definitely more than a few degrees off North.

"I shudder to think what your parents must be going through."

"Dad got a little cyclonic, but Mom said I could move back in with her."

"Is that so? And what are you going to do with yourself?"

He looked me straight in the eyes and said, "I'd like to create a paradise cocoon where people can go and transform themselves."

Liza, who had regained consciousness just in time to witness this heresy, blacked out again, and a small flower on her desk wilted.

"And how do you plan to manufacture this 'paradise cocoon' as you call it? Are plastics involved?"

He laughed. "I'm talkin' *music* here. The dudes I'm hangin' with are into electronica. You create these awesome sounds with computers. The network I've set up generates, like, all this random chaos that I massage into a garden of sound. It's way radical."

I tried to interrupt, but he continued animatedly, "There's this one guy, you wouldn't know him, but he takes the sounds of corporations he hates, you know, like McDonald's and Disney, and uses their own products to generate the noise that destroys them. He's got this track for Starbucks where there's the Frappuccino and then the toilet flushing. You should give it a listen."

"I'll put it on my Christmas list."

Nicholas had chosen to answer the pathetic siren call of the worst of his generation. There was nothing to do now but let him learn the hard way. I only hoped he wouldn't be bruised too badly. He was still young enough that he could make something of himself in five to ten years if his new way of life didn't become a habit. Nicholas retrieved a few personal items in his office, we shook hands, and he walked toward the door.

I gave it one last try. "You realize, of course, that you're giving up full dental coverage. Your teeth will go straight to hell."

"Oh, well, I can always play a creep on the *X-Files*."

"You had it made," I continued. "You could have retired here."

He gave me a puzzled look. "Time-Life is the only place handing out guarantees."

"There are plenty of guarantees right here if you work hard enough, and follow the rules."

"If only life was that simple," he sighed. "On second thought, I'm glad it's not."

"You're walking away from a bright financial future."

At that point, he simply thanked me for the opportunity and left.

I walked slowly back to my office to rue the senseless waste of what had once been so much potential. Take heed. Let my words be not only a source of counsel and a practical reference as you enter the business world—let this young man's careless descent also serve as a stern warning.

N: *Time To Fly*

I was suffocating in that cube farm. I had to get out. Man, did I get a kick out of showing up like that at the end! That was the most fun I ever had in that place.

There's been a lot of uncertainty in my life, so it really wasn't that big of a deal to leave. I know some of my parents' friends patted themselves on their backs for jumping ship and starting their own companies. I give them credit for that, but they were usually about 45 years old and had fat bank accounts to fall back on.

I didn't want to give up the loft and move back home, but there was no room for another roommate to help with expenses. I know it seems contradictory to head back to the nest when you're talking about *flying*, but what are the alternatives? Become a comatose "lifer" at Ablebright Manufacturing? Take a McJob to keep my apartment but little else? No, thanks.

"I would have bought a tent, camped in the woods, and ate squirrel meat before I moved back in with *my* parents," Hub told me.

That's part of that stubborn pride his generation is famous for. A double-edged sword if you ask me. I remember a story by Faulkner or somebody that I read in English Lit one year about this downtrodden old guy who never wanted to be "beholden" to anyone. His family had some problems and people wanted to help him out, but he kept refusing. They go through all this suffering for no reason.

And, by the way, Liza didn't actually pass out when I showed up, and I don't remember any lights flickering. Hub and his generation love to exaggerate. Watch for that.

MENTORING
THE
NEW EXECUTIVE

1

IN THE BEGINNING

H: *My Life*

Where should I start? How about in the beginning? How fondly I remember my youth.

I was born in humble surroundings to an upstanding and hard-working, middle-class family. My no-nonsense father kept food in our stomachs and clothes on our backs. My dutiful mother was buried in her apron. My older brothers handed their overalls down to me, taught me how to catch a catfish in the millpond, and showed me how to hit a baseball with a wooden bat in the sandlot down the street.

I was reared in a humble town where civic-minded neighbors swatted each other's kids if they got too uppity. Concerned folks sat outside on their porches with their arms folded and waited for the paperboy to pedal past. Then they'd scold him about the weather, the biting flies, the way he threw the paper, or his older brother's smart mouth—didn't matter what. He was a kid, and kids rightly needed scolding.

I learned the three "Rs" in a humble brick school within walking distance that was named after a Civil War general.

We scraped our knees on the concrete playground and burned the backs of our legs on the sun-baked aluminum slide, and every day begged the teacher for five minutes more. Math wasn't "new" yet and history wasn't "old" yet. When we lipped off, we got introduced to the "board of education," and we were better for it.

I attended a humble church every Sunday and was proud of my only good suit. My mother darned the holes so often the pants shrunk right up to my shins. I received gold stars for memorizing the names of the animals on the ark. Even today, decades later, I can still come back for a visit and hear the familiar hymns and the same comfortable liturgy, as if I never left.

I got my first humble job delivering groceries for tight-fisted Mr. Heebers. After high school, I spent six years selling shoes at Penney's, working my way up the old-fashioned way, from squeaky children's sneakers to flat-soled men's loafers to patented orthopedic boots. Thanks to a fortunate series of re-tirements I eventually found myself upstairs in the manager's office. From there I went on to a variety of managerial and ex-ecutive positions until finally founding my own company at the age of 51, where I remained until my recent retirement. In short, I am an experienced businessman, having stood on the firing line every day, my feet firmly planted in the real world.

N: *How . . . Quaint*
Sounds like Mayberry, except that Hub forgot to mention the lovable town drunk.

H: *Your Life*
You, of course, as a member of a more recent generation, have had a markedly less blessed upbringing. With my help, you can overcome it.

You were probably born in an anonymous daycare facility. Your mother was out snatching good jobs away from men who needed them, and before long she was living it up as a divorcée, and you were left wearing a latchkey around your neck. Instead of sturdy hand-me-downs, you were stuck with poorly manufactured fashions from the strip mall across town. The only fishing you ever did was at a fish farm, and the only "bat" anybody taught you how to swing was a plastic joystick.

None of your neighbors were ever home in your neighborhood, a place that consisted of porch-less suburban homes and a cigarette-infested 7-Eleven, where you loitered outside and learned what you could about life and sex. The paperboy was either a teenage dropout who delivered the paper if he felt like it or an ex-con who drove an old beater and did well to get the Sunday paper onto your doorstep by noon.

For your education, you were bussed to a fancy but sterile new school named after a local liberal on the far edge of town. Your muscles turned to flab as you refused to play on wood chips and plastic purple slides. Math was something you faked on a calculator and history meant events from last week. Teachers got sued if they so much as looked at a kid sternly.

If you attended church, it was probably one that met in an arena and featured electric guitars and a hip youth pastor who told you how "cool" Jesus was. Of course, you were never made to wear a suit—they figured it was enough of a sacrifice for you to tuck in the front of your shirt. The Ten Commandments gathered dust while wishy-washy adults told you to trust your feelings.

After high school, you were handed your first job at a place like McDonald's, which, due to a demographically dwindling labor pool, had to bribe you with tuition reimbursements, free meals, and uniforms. Then you went off to college and had the nerve to expect a high-paying position immediately upon receiving your degree.

N: *Graduation And Beyond*

How did we ever survive?! I guess I'll pick up the story where Hub left off. At the graduation job fair we faced one of two scenarios, depending on the state of the economy: The "boom" fair or the "bust" fair.

At the boom fair, with the economy soaring, all of the companies were hiring and the competition for graduates was fierce. The exhibit hall was filled with bright, colorful booths jammed together. Balloons with logos floated around a whirling disco ball, and a brass band paraded up and down the aisles. (That was supposed to impress us.) Tanned babes clad in bikinis or jungle cloths handed out company freebies as they hung from the booths. Some companies brought in has-been bands to sign copies of their last CD and sing the company motto a cappella.

The bust fair was a different scene altogether. A recession threatened, and almost no companies were hiring. The door to the empty exhibit hall echoed as it slammed shut behind us. In the dim light we identified what appeared to be a lone booth in one of the shadowy corners. We made our way across the vast floor, brushing aside cobwebs, until we arrived at the booth. Behind it sat a glassy-eyed Army recruiter mumbling imaginary orders to attack the Vietcong. A cardboard cutout of Sylvester Stallone stood nearby commanding us to buy recruitment videos for $24.99.

H: *What's Next?*

One thing is sure: No matter what type of economy you faced after graduation, you've probably maxed out your credit cards. If you haven't found a real job yet, you're still in need of some tips on resumes and interviews. If you have begun a career, you will need advice on the ways of the business world— especially how to get ahead. In either case, you've come to the right place.

Heaven knows, Nicholas could have benefited from a book such as this. He was unprepared for the corporate culture and never did adapt. Early in his tenure I happened to overhear a phone conversation he had in his office cubicle.

"Melanie, you can't believe how rigid it is here. I mean, like, you can't even wear your sunglasses in your own cube. Plus, I have to be here six months before I can take a day off . . . yeah, I know. What if Linkin Park is touring—I'm just supposed to skip it?. . . And the people here are so uptight—like their heads are going to explode if you don't file everything in the exact right place. . . . Then, I went out for lunch and came back five minutes late, and my manager went ballistic, like I was some kind of mass murderer."

You, however, can know what to expect in advance. Whether you take the necessary steps to conform is up to you, but at least my hands will be clean.

2

RESUMES

N: *Surprising Opposition*

Creating a resume is a big deal. It signals to our friends and parents that we really are serious about quitting that garage band and pursuing our careers—which probably means leaving town and living someplace far away. Most parents react with barely concealed enthusiasm toward this turn of events, but some mothers—especially from small-town families—become hesitant as they realize one of their "babies" is departing the nest for a few years. These moms, transformed into representatives of the local chamber of commerce, may even stand in the doorway and attempt to persuade their son or daughter to stay.

"Why would you want to leave Blandton?" Mom will start off. "Everything you need is right here. It's safe. There are good schools, and they're starting a computer club down at the senior center—you could volunteer to teach classes. Wouldn't that be fun?"

"Mom, I've got a degree in business. I want a real job in a real city."

"Well, they're always looking for new agents down at the State Farm office."

"Mom!"

"There's nothing wrong with selling insurance. Your uncle did it for years."

"I know, but . . ."

Then dad lifts his head over the newspaper. "All that college was a waste anyway. You could've been a plumber by now, earning good money. You never see them looking for work."

By this point, the kid can't wait to get that resume in the mailbox.

H: *Sorely Lacking*

Well, it's about time you put something in the mailbox. You can't just sail around on the good ship *Lollygag* forever.

I had no need to put together a resume or leave town in my early years, because several local stores offered me positions even before I graduated. Nevertheless, those of you who are not as lucky will need to prepare this formal advertisement to the world that you are qualified—or at least available—for work.

Judging from the content of the resumes that I have reviewed, the instructions that aspiring young professionals receive about resume preparation has been sorely lacking. Your contemporaries, in their constant efforts to display their diversity and independence, seem to have adopted their own rules for grammar, spelling, punctuation, and overall presentation. If not for some companies lowering their standards, few of these lax and indifferent applicants would be hired.

I have even heard that some companies now accept resumes in languages other than English. What's next? Resumes from the illiterate that use pictures instead of words? When companies cater to the lowest denominator, that is exactly what they get.

N: *Lighten Up*

Regarding grammar and all that stuff—hey, I thought English was a "living" language. It's there to serve *us*, right? Not the other way around. If every generation strictly conformed, we'd still speaketh like Shakespeare.

H: *Pointers For A Strong Resume*

Though I never had to do a resume, I can still offer plenty of tips based on the dozens of resumes that crossed my desk from prospective employees every month.

1) **Include current contact information.**

Unless you want to rely on your vagabond roommates to forward your mail, you should probably double-check your resume before sending it out to make sure your address and phone number are correct. If you move around a lot and your girlfriend isn't always available for retyping, you might want to try making a number of copies of your resume *without* the contact information. Then you can have your latest address typed in when the need arises.

2) **Freshen it up every few years.**

When you first prepared your resume way back when, it might have been a real feather in your cap that you handled logistics for an Internet grocer. Since they've all gone belly up, the luster of that assignment has worn off a bit. Have your girlfriend white out that section so you can replace it with something fresher. You might also want to take another look at the hobbies you listed. Following the DEAF Jam tour around the country may show perseverance, but that image is not the one you want.

3) **Take a conservative approach.**

I don't care what your moony friends say about a resume on purple stationery being more expressive and spiritual. Such shenanigans are doomed to failure. Managers aren't looking for creative spirits—they want people who can take orders.

The most absurd resume I ever received came inside six successive packages, each one slightly smaller than the one before. On the outermost box was a note that read, "I'm worth the effort." Thinking there was something exciting inside, my heart rate increased with each box I opened. Imagine my disappointment and disgust when I opened the final box and found nothing more than some clown's resume.

4) **Proofread it.**

Your unemployed buddy will probably tell you something along the lines of, "If that manager dude reviewing your resume gets so paranoid about a couple trivial mistakes, you probably don't want to work for him anyway." Don't worry, you won't.

5) Try to fill the page.

The hard truth is, a resume that's mostly a blank sheet of paper doesn't make the kind of statement you need. Maybe you've tried using larger type and extra spaces. This might be hard to believe, but you've got more to offer than you realize. If you once set aside your video games and had a paper route for a week one summer, or you handled the hose at a charity car wash at church, mention it. You never know which experiences will strike a chord with the reviewer. At the very least, you will fill up that page.

6) Don't boast about what ought to be forgotten.

There's an opposite extreme to the problem facing the inexperienced applicants discussed in #5. It's the misguided notion that failure in business is good—a learning experience—and therefore a real advantage that a candidate should trumpet. I can't remember where I read it, but one of the failed dot-commers claimed he felt "blessed by tragedy." Let me be clear on this right now. You're blessed by *success and prosperity*—don't let anybody con you into believing anything different.

7) Avoid words and phrases you might think are impressive but in reality only turn veteran managers off.

Examples: *Digital, network certified, dialogic space modeling, sociocultural capacity building, community impact assessment, context sensitive solutions, mediated consensus analysis, nurtured.*

8) Use fast-action verbs and impressive adjectives.

I suggest verbs such as *spearheaded, bulldozed, strongarmed, bullied, rammed, dropkicked, plundered, commandeered, whipped,* and *pounced.* Adjectives may include *extraordinary, dominant, global, crowning, preeminent, divine, anointed,* and *humble.*

N: *Hub's Pointers Revisited*

Personally, I thought the applicant who sent his resume inside those six boxes should have at least been given points for creativity. Several of us in the office had gathered around to see what all the commotion was about.

"We don't need creativity here," Hub, who had worked up a lather, lectured us. "We manufacture parts for lawn mowers, remember?"

"I thought new ideas were a good thing," I ventured.

"Who told you that?" he foamed, pointing his finger at me. "Let me give you a little heads up. You don't make money selling 'new ideas.' You make money by selling what's tried-and-true. We don't have to come up with laser lawn mowers to be successful. All we have to do is provide the market standard at reasonable prices and with reasonable service."

"But wouldn't it be better if someone came up with a way that people didn't have to mow lawns in the first place?"

"Ah, the idealism of youth," said Harry Baxter, one of the bad-breathed, graying VPs, who had joined the group.

Hub laughed and whispered to Harry, "Next, they'll start saying we should manufacture stronger parts so the mowers will last longer!"

A couple of days later, I was reviewing resumes with Hub for a new hire in my department.

"This one's no good," Hub remarked, tossing the resume aside. "He forgot a comma."

I grabbed it quickly off the pile. "But he had the best qualifications of anyone," I said.

"You still need to learn what managers and corporations value."

I'm learning all right. Creativity isn't that important to executives like Hub, because it hasn't been a necessity. They've had so much wealth and such abundant resources that they simply throw piles of money and brute force at whatever problems come along until they "succeed." It goes all of the way back to a well-funded Edison starting out with huge steam engines in neighborhood power stations and miles of wiring all over the place like spaghetti. What if he hadn't had the resources to implement such a labor and material-intensive strategy? Maybe he might have been more creative (like you and I are going to have to be), and wireless power would have been born instead.

H: *Resume Padding*

I'd better move on before Nicholas starts babbling about FedEx and UPS "beaming" packages from one place to another.

The U.S. Census Bureau has added a new category to its demographic data for educational attainment levels:

> ▶ No high school diploma or GED
> ▶ High school diploma or GED
> ▶ Two-year college or technical degree

> ► Four-year college degree
>> ► Graduate degree
>> ► Fudged resume

What is my take on the "resume padding" trend? Pundits have traced it to everything from the "Bill Clinton effect" to low self-esteem. These explanations are way off base. The reality is my generation of stellar achievers has set such a high standard of excellence that less experienced professionals feel intimidated. Consequently, professionals seeking management- and executive-level positions add phony accomplishments to their resumes in desperate attempts to measure up.

N: *Who's Padding?*

There's just one problem with Hub's theory. Most of the resume "padders," at least the ones in the news, have been over 40. Turns out they didn't have that degree after all. Most blame it on poor memory! One even went so far as to say she had always thought she had earned enough credits for her bachelor's degree. Say what? Last time I checked there were these little things called graduation and a diploma that usually tend to remove all doubt.

It amazes me that the very same human resource managers who scrutinize every comma on my resume are the same ones who don't even bother to check major credentials for older, upper management candidates.

H: *References*

Rest assured, references *are* checked. Using family members is unacceptable for obvious reasons—so sorry, you can't use your dad, even though he may seem like nothing more than an acquaintance. Your friend who graduated six months before you did and has been a manager trainee for three weeks now is no good, either. Also avoid judges and attorneys, even if your relationship is outside the courtroom.

What about your dentist? Well, I know they say you can tell a lot about a horse by its teeth, but I doubt whether it works for humans. Your mailman? Yes, he's handled most of your personal documents and important papers over the years, but the reputation of postal workers has been tarnished. Your girlfriend? Don't even consider it. What if you had a fight the night before they call her? You know how emotional girls are. She'd probably scream something like, "You can have that spineless bum!" Even under the best of circumstances she's liable to blurt out inappropriate questions such as, "How much money would he make?" or "How old would his secretary be?"

Ideally, you should try to track down a professor who's not on sabbatical or a distracted business manager (maybe your friend's dad—if there are no hard feelings about that time with his car).

Whatever you do, make sure to alert your references beforehand. When the first thing out of the mouth of your reference is "Who?" in response to the personnel manager's inquiry about you, your chances generally suffer (although some candidates might be better off using references who *don't* know them).

N: *Why Use References At All?*

Too often the business world does things because "That's the way it's always been done." Providing references is a perfect example. Everyone knows at least three people who are going to say nice things about them—what does that prove? Plus, even human resource experts admit that for legal reasons the questions that can be asked and the answers that can be given are few. Vague generalities are all that's going to be exchanged. Why bother?

When I'm thinking of working with someone, I just cruise the Web or the newsgroups. I can usually find out just about anything on anyone.

H: *Cover Letters*

Too bad you can't find out how to *write* on the Internet. A common complaint toward your generation is that you've lost the art of letter writing. (Let's not kid ourselves, you've lost the art of *any* kind of writing.) Hence, for you a cover letter is aptly named: Any letters you write ought to remain under a cover. Dig a few crumpled bucks out of the trousers lying on your floor and pay a professional to write the letter that accompanies your resume.

3

INTERVIEWS

H: *A Formal Occasion*

Interviews are a critical part of the career building process—you can't afford to leave them to chance. You don't want to miss out on a plum job because you laid an egg in the interview room.

Occasionally, I would sit in on an interview for a new entry-level manager, as I happened to do in Nicholas' case. He performed better than most, which is perhaps one of the reasons I later took an interest in his progress.

Many young greenhorns are poorly prepared for a formal setting like the interview room. They prefer that every situation be *informal*, with no difference between a skateboard rally and a royal wedding. I have seen too many uncombed heads, pierced noses, invisible ties, and cheap loafers. The image projected is one of detached indifference—occasionally even disrespect. My hunch is, these individuals feel safer when they pretend not to care. Then, failure doesn't hurt as much. Unfortunately, they are setting themselves up for the very failure they fear. No wonder the incomes of the next generation are projected to lag behind the levels of previous ones. This need not happen to you!

N: *A Formal Complaint*
It's so awesome to continually be judged by how you look!

H: *Being Interviewed*
Appearance counts, because most interviewers can only draw
from a canned stock of questions that the personnel manager has
deemed harmless enough to avoid legal action. Since this leaves
very few possible questions, it is easy to anticipate what will be
asked, and prepare strong responses. Some standard questions
and my recommended answers follow.

"Why should I hire you?"
WEAK RESPONSE: "Because I'm a hard worker, and I really need
this job." (Here's your lovely parting gift. Desperation never gets
you anywhere.)
STRONG RESPONSE: "Because you deserve the best. This isn't
about me, it's about the company continuing to improve itself." (Great answer—even if we know you're kidding.)

"Describe one of your weak points."
WEAK: (Any answer that tells the truth.)
STRONG: "Because I have the ability to work smarter not harder,
it often looks to others like I'm not doing much. This sometimes
leads to jealousy among my co-workers when I am promoted before them." (This answer is ideal, because it covers your daily performance whether you accomplish anything or not.)

"What are your strong points?"
WEAK: "I'm a real team player." (Save the corporate babble for
the next feel-good seminar. Team players only get off the bench
to bunt.)
STRONG: "I'm very good at following the examples of my superiors and learning from them." (That's the only strong point you'll
need.)

"Can you make quick decisions?"
WEAK: "I prefer to study a matter first, get input from others affected by the decision, and then make the best choice." (Better
hope you're allowed a mulligan.)

STRONG: "Make me an offer and you'll find out." (Decisive. Snappy.)

"I see you had a part-time job. Did you work your way through college?"
WEAK: "Yes, I'm very proud of that." (*Anybody* can work his way through college.)

STRONG: "I worked for one semester so I could buy up some blue chippers while they were low." (Besides the statement this makes about your background, it tells prospective employers you're fresh, not burned out.)

"What gives you the most job satisfaction?"
WEAK: "Helping others do their best." (Do we look like the United Way here?)

STRONG: "Making as much money as I can, because then I have more resources to help others." (Try to look serious when you say that second part.)

"Why did you leave your last job?"
WEAK: "Actually, I'm still at the deli." (Pathetic.)

STRONG: "It was time for me to step up to the big leagues." (Go grab a bat, slugger.)

"Would you mind taking a lie-detector test?"
WEAK: "No, not at all." (You just took one, and you failed.)

STRONG: "Wouldn't that be a waste of the Fifth Amendment?" (A solid knowledge of American history is always a plus.)

"Where do you see yourself five years from now?"
WEAK: "At my current pace I should be on my fifth job by then. Or, I might be back in school working on a new degree." (This may be typical, but you don't have to admit it!)

STRONG: "I'm impressed with the company's mission statement. I see myself developing a long career here in direct harmony with those values." (Because the manager conducting the interview usually can't remember what his company's mission statement says, this will temporarily knock him off balance. When he recovers, however, he's bound to be impressed by your preparation.)

N: *Job-Hopping*

Five years is a long time—how should we know where we're going to be?

"Job-hopping is becoming a serious problem," Hub bellowed at an employee meeting one day.

"They claim it broadens their experiences and helps them grow," Harry Baxter chimed in.

"How am I supposed to train a successor? And how is anyone ever going to become vested?"

Several younger employees sitting in the room wore puzzled expressions. I'm guessing they were wondering what "vested" meant. Derek from logistics leaned over and whispered, "Does that have anything to do with wearing a sweater vest, like Baxter?"

"Yes," I said. "Even in the summer."

"Buttoned all the way to the top?"

"Yeah."

Hub rose from his seat, buttoned his suit jacket, and stepped toward the front of the group. While Hub cleared his throat, Harry hustled over and dimmed the lights in the back so that the ones in front shone on Hub like a spotlight. We gripped our chairs and braced ourselves for another windy monologue. When Hub got wound up and the hot air started blowing, it was like being in a wind tunnel. The faces of people sitting in the front rows became all distorted like those test pilots encountering G-forces head-on.

"The true cause of this situation is the world of unlimited choices that has opened up around you young people in the past few decades. Up until the 1850's, people could wear their shoes on either foot. When I was growing up, young men had a few simple choices to make: Join the army, work on the farm, take a job at the factory, or take over their father's business. Young women either married and raised families or became nurses or school teachers. There were three television channels to watch and two flavors of Kool-Aid. Fewer options meant less time agonizing over choices and fewer regrets later. Now, you grow up with hundreds of cable stations and Snapple gives you a choice of flavors ranging from 'Arctic Pineapple' to 'Green Banana.'"

Derek slid lower in his chair and put his hand over the label on his Snapple bottle.

"Then, one day, off you go to any one of several colleges, where you must eventually choose between dozens of majors. After graduation, you receive job offers from all over the country. Is it any wonder you can't stay in one place? There's always a nagging feeling inside that you're missing something somewhere else. You can't help but grab the remote and change the channel of your life to see what it's like at that other company."

"Oh, but we love it here, Mr. Ablebright. We'd never think of going anywhere else," said a perky human resource assistant.

That was hardly the end of Hub's lecture, but that's about all I can remember. Anyway, here's my angle on the job-hopping trend. Companies expect you to stick with them long-term, which is understandable, but not very realistic. They seem to hold it against employees who consider leaving for a more attractive offer. And, yet, what else can a company expect when it hires talented people? Of course they're going to be in demand. That's the risk a company takes for hiring the best. Companies could always settle for the alternative: Hire people who are either 1) so inept that they'll never receive another offer, or 2) too lacking in ambition to accept another offer when it does come.

H: *When You're The Interviewer*

Let's imagine that you've managed to stay at one company long enough to gain a promotion. Now *you're* the one putting others on the hot seat. As an interviewer, there are several questions you want to ask but can't due to "politically correct" federal and state laws. You need to know certain information—what do you do? You must learn how to rephrase questions to help the interviewees disclose information on their own. Some examples follow.

NEED TO KNOW: Is the longhaired blonde applicant willing to do whatever it takes to ensure her success?
CAN'T ASK: "How did you fare on the 'Hottie Board' at your previous employer?"
CAN'T ASK: "Have you had your tubes tied?" (No good, even if you claim you're asking for insurance purposes.)
ALTERNATIVE: Tell her she needs to fill out an application, then hand her the thickest pen you have. See what she does with it.

NEED TO KNOW: Is the interviewee one of those troublesome "women's libbers"?
CAN'T ASK: "If you're hired here full-time, who's going to watch your kids?"
CAN'T ASK: "Why do you have a hyphenated last name?"
ALTERNATIVE: Arrange two chairs at the table (besides your own). When she enters the room, does she take the chair you pull out for her?

NEED TO KNOW: Does the interviewee belong to some oddball religious or political group?
CAN'T ASK: "Does that goatee mean anything?"
CAN'T ASK: "Would you like to begin with a chant or small animal sacrifice?"
ALTERNATIVE: "We're a very benevolent organization—never turn anyone down. While you're here, if you have any requests just let my secretary know before you leave."

NEED TO KNOW: How old is the prospective employee anyway?
CAN'T ASK: "Would you like Milk of Magnesia with your coffee?"
CAN'T ASK: "Do you anticipate living long enough to pass our six-month probationary period?"
ALTERNATIVE: Try to get him to talk about his grandkids—*that* shouldn't be too difficult. Once you gain enough information to discern the kids' ages, you'll have a good idea of how old grandpa is.

N: *Too Structured*
This whole interview thing seems so forced and phony. I'd rather toss all my potential business partners into a mosh pit, and see how they react. That's where a person's true nature comes out.

H: *Lasting Impression*
Nowadays, people think the way to leave a lasting impression is to make fools of themselves. Run naked across the field at a college football game. Bite the head off a bat at a concert. Spill your family secrets on a sleazy talk show. Marry a stranger on national television (then divorce him on *Court TV*). *Anything* for that fifteen minutes of fame.

Business—and life—is not about fleeting fame. It is about putting your nose to the grindstone and being consistently dependable day after day. Companies need workers who are willing to dedicate their lives to doing the ordinary things that need doing. These are not things that will get you on *Good Morning America*, but they will keep this country strong and productive. Likewise, when you start a family your wife and children will need you to provide a steady paycheck, kill the dandelions in the lawn, and keep the rain gutters clean—let somebody else waste their time trying to become the next American idol.

You can make your case for consistency during the interview by showing up on time, providing solid references, and answering the questions with the standard replies. Believe me, if you just do these three things, you *will* stand out, because so few applicants today seem able to meet this standard.

Nicholas almost blew it during his interview when he tried to make a splash by responding to a question with what he probably thought was a clever answer.

"I'd rather try to achieve something really special and fail," he said, "than settle for mediocrity."

I interrupted the personnel manager conducting the interview. "Well, young man, it might surprise you to know that a company that shared your philosophy would go bankrupt right quick."

"But there's a chance I wouldn't fail—then I'd be the leader in a totally new field."

"Look, son, successful businessmen *manage* risk—they don't go encouraging it. The fat may be on the edge, but the meat is in the middle."

Afterward the personnel manager showed me something Nicholas had written in small letters on the back of his application: "The phat is on the edge!"

"Well, he can't spell, but at least he finally got it," I said.

4

OFFICE CHARACTERS

H: *First Day*

Your first day at work finds you in one of three scenarios: 1) a sprawling corporate campus with dozens of buildings and thousands of employees, 2) a mid-sized company complex with a handful of buildings and maybe a few hundred employees, or 3) the single building of a firm with less than 100 employees. The professional culture differs among these scenarios to some degree, but their similarities far outnumber their differences.

Though upon your arrival you first notice landscaped flagpoles, curving green lawns, and airy atriums, it is ultimately the people working inside that will come to represent the face of the company. How you deal with individual relationships will determine your success or failure.

People exhibit a limited number of personality types. Stereotyping, which has gotten a bad rap recently, is actually a useful and practical tool. Office politics is all about recognizing these personalities and managing them accordingly.

I distinctly remember the day Nicholas came to work for me. In contrast to the detached expression he wore on his last day, his introduction was characterized by a wide-eyed curiosity. He was, of course, fresh meat—in desperate need of coaching. Unfortunately, very few companies have the time or resources to spare to get greenhorns up to speed. Consider yourself extra fortunate to hold in your hands a guide like the one I have laid out for you on the next few pages.

N: *A Blur*

I don't remember much of my first day. Looking back, though, I can now see that many of the first impressions I formed turned out to be wrong. People and places aren't always what you think they are.

H: *The Cast Of Characters And How To Deal With Them*

SNARLER (Pit Bull)

Personality: Aggressive. Persistent. Irritating. Rude.

Appearance: Short hair or a bald, "sharp" head. Walks fast. Stares people down. A menace in the company parking lot, his truck always has at least one dent in it.

Activities: This antagonist is usually in "attack" mode. No policy, institution, or person is spared his biting criticism. Usually too angry to eat lunch. Livid if his stocks don't go up every day and his football team doesn't cover the spread.

My Advice: I gained a fair measure of respect and prestige among the employees because I was one of the few people strong enough to take on this bully. Young professionals from your generation are likely to be intrigued at first by Pit Bull's disregard for all things—but it will quickly become apparent that his disregard includes your generation, too. ("A bunch of slackers!") You'd best let the big boys handle this character.

BACKSTABBER (Snake)

Personality: Sly. Conniving. Dishonest. Insecure.

Appearance: Long, thin tongue. Saccharin smile and lukewarm handshake. Notes others' gaffes at lunch and office parties for future reference.

Activities: Starts by getting something trashy on the office gossip, then strong-arms her for inside information. Gains trust of unwitting associates by appearing to confess his weaknesses. The juicy secrets colleagues share are later used against them.

My Advice: This viper did a lot of my dirty work for me. Just kidding! Nicholas spotted our Snakes surprisingly quickly, though I'm not sure how. At any rate, be careful whom you trust.

MS. LAWSUIT (Vulture)

Personality: Picky. Observant. Litigious.

Appearance: Always dressed as if for a court appearance. Drives a different employee's former car every month.

Activities: Tape records her job interview. Had an internship as a paralegal and likes to pass herself off as an attorney. Always tossing around terms like "settle," "deposition," and "just cause." Specializes in internal OSHA violations and sexual harassment.

My Advice: I played along with the lawyer act and put her on retainer. It's the only way I could keep myself out of court, since she wouldn't sue her own client.

TOO QUIET (Termite)

Personality: Shy. Never speaks up. Overly educated.

Appearance: Wears plain clothing. Seldom makes eye contact and squints when he does. Cable hanging from pants pocket is connected to a computer somewhere. Doesn't seem to own a car— just appears suddenly out of the shadows and disappears silently again into the bowels of the building.

Activities: No one knows for sure. The damage is being done while you sleep. Then, one day, your gutted company implodes.

My Advice: This guy worried me. Trouble is, he always got his work done and never caused commotion, so I seldom had a direct reason to fire him. (Even when I did have a reason, I couldn't find him.)

NONCONFORMIST (Cat)

Personality: Independent. Stubborn. Often just plain odd.

Appearance: Eccentric clothing and grooming. Far-away expression. Eats lunch alone.

Activities: You give him precise instructions, he nods blankly, and then he goes out and does something totally different. Prefers Apple computers, NASDAQ stocks, vegetarian meals, and rooting against the USA in the Olympics.

My Advice: I never trusted this guy. You'd see these oddballs on the golf course by themselves and they'd always play the holes out of sequence. I've seen a few young professionals turn into these types after a year or two, so watch yourself.

MS. ENVY (Hyena)
Personality: Nosey. Petty. Frustrated. Bitter.
Appearance: Green is her favorite color. Wears expensive looking outfits. Fascinated by her own well-manicured hands. Leases the latest car models and pretends to own each one.
Activities: Used to fight with her siblings over who got the banana with the label on it. Just like family fights, most discrimination lawsuits are initiated by nothing more than envy. She is constantly on the lookout for who got promoted, how much of a raise everybody got, and who gets to park in the "reserved" stalls up front.
My Advice: We lions will always have our hyenas on the fringe. I accepted it as confirmation that I had achieved a status and compensation level that merited the envy of others. You probably won't give her much to be envious about for several years, so don't worry about her.

LADDER CLIMBER (Monkey)
Personality: Assertive. Impatient. Energetic. Appears friendly on the surface.
Appearance: Smartly dressed. Styled hair. Quick smile. Drives more car than he can afford.
Activities: First thing he wants to know at his job interview is how many months it took the manager interviewing him to get to his position. This fellow has one thing on his mind: Getting ahead, and he'll do anything to advance. Continually buys and dumps stocks, trying to make a quick killing.
My Advice: I liked this type because he's productive. I strapped administrative weights around him to slow his climb and keep him in my office for as long as possible. Your generation could use a bit more of Monkey's ambition, so observe him carefully whenever you can.

DO-IT-ALL (Octopus)
Personality: Busy. Bossy. Feels under-appreciated.

Appearance: Somehow stays neat and clean despite the constant demands of the day.

Activities: Has her tentacles in everything. Is convinced the company could not function properly without her. Will re-file, re-contact, re-word, re-organize, re-check, and re-process just about everything you do to ensure all of it is done to her standards.

My Advice: Octopus will stir up a fuss about being overworked. When you lay another assignment on her desk she may even roll her eyes and mumble, "I don't know when I'm going to get to this, but I'll fit it in somewhere." But try taking some responsibility away from her and she will react as though you are cutting off one of her tentacles.

KNOW-IT-ALL (Owl)

Personality: Pompous. Learned. Dull.

Appearance: Gray-bearded and balding on top. Wears round glasses. Double chinned. Drinks tea. Mensa bumper sticker on his Volvo.

Activities: Reclines in his high-backed armchair with his hands clasped behind his head and dispenses wisdom to all who enter his office. Can occasionally be found at meetings or conferences pontificating to the masses. Used to teach college classes until he received his third doctorate, after which he was deemed too educated to teach—nobody could understand him anymore. Draws regular attention to his many obscure publishing credits in *The Journal of Inordinately High Intelligence* and *Super Genius Illustrated*. Likes to take credit for insights that are after-the-fact, such as how he knew all along that the stock market was going to fall/rise.

My Advice: Don't be too impressed. I always came away with "more than I wanted to know" from this chap. If he's so wise, why is it that half of the staff in marketing earns twice as much as he does? The pencil sharpener in his office broke down once, and he was so bewildered he had to call in the oaf from maintenance.

BABBLER-WITH-A-CAUSE (Turkey)

Personality: Self-righteous. Zealous. Much too dedicated.

Appearance: High brows. Thin lips. Wears advocacy buttons on lapel.

Activities: Leaves basement-printed tracts in the lunchroom that attempt to enlighten the world about Hare Krishna, Joe Camel, natural childbirth, Teletubbies, or some other cause. Sprinkles the cause's latest cliches into every conversation at the slightest opportunity. You (innocently): "Hey, did you hear Eric Burdon is reuniting The Animals?" The Turkey (furiously): "Animals have the same rights as people!"

My Advice: Several female employees in need of discipline at home once gathered in the parking lot by my car to shout, "I am Woman, hear me roar!" Since they obviously had too much time on their hands, I instructed their managers to double their workload the next morning.

COMPLAINER (Crow)
Personality: Annoying voice. Constantly finding fault.

Appearance: No distinguishing features—can apply to just about anyone these days. Loves a captive audience, so tries to ride with someone else to work.

Activities: Is extremely good-natured at her interview—these types never start complaining until *after* they're hired. Eats in the company cafeteria every day because it's such an easy target. Whines about her small cubicle, her uncomfortable chair, the temperature in the office, and especially her boss. Even complains about bonuses, no matter how generous. If a man, he likes to regularly gripe about the return on his 401(k) and tell everybody how much more he could have made investing the money himself.

My Advice: I always wanted to send these types to my competitors so they could see how good they had it under my care. After the initial glow wears off, it's easy for young professionals to become cynical, especially since it comes so naturally to a generation reared on the likes of Beavis & Butt-Head.

EXAGGERATOR (Rooster)
Personality: Animated. Loud. Loves the limelight.

Appearance: Oversized mouth in relation to rest of head. Wears "knock-off" suits. Every lunch is the best he's ever eaten. Drives a car that gets "at least 70 mpg" on the highway.

Activities: Blows everything out of proportion. He claims his staff "has the talent of tree stumps but gets paid like oil sheiks—

it's amazing I haven't gone insane." His three (maybe he only has two) kids are either constantly on the verge of landing in prison or winning the Nobel Prize.

My Advice: At the last annual shareholder's meeting, after I nudged the live donkey out onto the stage and told the troops we were going to "kick ass," I marched this guy up to the podium and let him rave about the health of the company.

EASILY OFFENDED (Horse)
Personality: Mood can change in an instant.

Appearance: Average looking, but will occasionally dress up (or down) to test your reaction.

Activities: This person looks for any reason to start neighing, in hopes of setting you off on a guilt trip and subsequent elaborate activities to get back in her good graces. I remember one Horse who made a big show of not having been invited to my office for a tour when she was hired. I finally invited her in one morning, closed the door, and left for the day.

My Advice: Be careful. I remember a touchy girl Friday who didn't talk to me for weeks after I complimented her on a new outfit she was wearing—turned out she had worn the stupid thing once before. (If only I could shut off my wife's spigot that easily.)

GADABOUT (Parrot)
Personality: An unabashed socialite who has to be right in the middle of everything.

Appearance: Wears the latest fashions. Uses too much makeup. Shares rides to get the latest gossip. Wherever you may wander on the corporate campus, you will invariably find your office Gadabout around the next corner.

Activities: For her the only purposes of employment are to socialize, decorate, and plan parties for every occasion (retirements, birthdays, promotions, flu shots). No holiday is too obscure. Eventually you won't even ask anymore why there are seven stuffed dwarves on the front counter and gingerbread men for treats in the break room (it's National Fairy Tales Week).

My Advice: I used Gadabouts both to obtain confidential information and to spread my own misinformation. A word of warning: In addition to their well-exercised tongues they also have very sensitive eyes and ears. This is important to remember when you are talking about something you don't want repeated. Having learned the hard way, I stuffed a towel between the carpeting and the door to prevent sound from escaping, and I stayed away from windows when speaking because Gadabouts are also talented lip readers.

DOUBLE-JOBBER (Ant)
Personality: High-strung. Preoccupied. Secretive.
Appearance: Often dressed improperly for an office setting. Walks around with a pencil stuck behind his ear. Drives a cargo van.
Activities: In addition to his regular job in your company, he is also clandestinely running his own private business out of his office. Unusual phone calls, faxes, deliveries, and visitors are the rule. He takes vacation in two-hour increments and frequently calls in sick. Most often slips up when he hands clients the wrong business card or forgets to take his safety goggles off.
My Advice: I discovered one division manager who was selling HVAC out of his office. When I confronted him, Ant offered me a great deal on a furnace and even threw in one of the water heaters he had stored in the company garage, so I went easy on him.

SUCK-UP (Sturgeon)
Personality: Alert for opportunities. Very flexible.
Appearance: Thick lips. Moist, nasally voice.
Activities: Also known as "brown-noser," "arse-licker," "apple-polisher." These folks flatter, pamper, and cater to important people either because they are trying to win points and get ahead, or they have no self-esteem and take some kind of perverse joy in humiliating themselves.
My Advice: Your generation needs to accept that there's nothing wrong with a little sucking up. However, Sturgeon goes too far and loses all dignity. But why complain? If somebody wanted to go into debt buying me free tickets to the big game, or shoveling a path through the snow to my car, I let them indulge themselves. What got old, however, was when they did things like convert from their religion to mine so they could spend an hour on Sundays with me, too.

SUNDIALER (Sloth)

Personality: Extremely laid back. No sense of urgency.

Appearance: Slow, deliberate movements and speech.

Activities: This guy can take a project that should last a day or two, and turn it into a month-long affair. If he had been in charge of Columbus' expedition, they'd just now be setting sail. The amazing thing is, he doesn't goof off or intentionally waste time— he just manages to find the longest distance between two points. He meant to get in on Enron when it was on its way to $90 a share, but by the time he pulled the trigger, it had dropped to 61 cents.

My Advice: A Sloth is excellent for slowing down Ladder Climber Monkey, so I tried to put them together on the same projects.

HANGER-ON (Bat)

Personality: Arthritic. Senile. Stale.

Appearance: Odor of mothballs surrounds him. Drives a 1968 AMC Rambler.

Activities: Should have retired years ago, but hangs on 1) "to keep myself out of trouble," or 2) under the delusion that he's still useful. Can't keep up with the Gadabout Parrot, so sets up shop in the lobby and gets in people's hair. Tells the same story five times every day about how he remembers when the company got its start in a cozy office next door to a funeral parlor, and if not for the smell he wishes the company was still there today. Still holding onto his shares of Wang Computer.

My Advice: If I ever become like this, I just pray somebody has the guts to close the lid.

CLOWN (Otter)

Personality: Playful. Full of jokes and pranks.

Appearance: Slightly disheveled, goofy look. Hitchhikes to work just to have a story to tell.

Activities: Stands near the copier half of the day telling jokes and stories. Overloads email server with silly photos and phony insider trading tips. Adjusts the water fountain so it squirts unsuspecting users. Career ends when "super" prank backfires and the sprinkler system goes off in Snarler Pit Bull's office.

My Advice: I tired of these types rather quickly, so I seldom stepped in when they wore out their welcome.

SPORTS GUY (Puppy)

Personality: Fun-loving. Shallow. Preoccupied.

Appearance: Tanned. Wears cuff links from the NCAA Final Four. Rides a motorcycle to work.

Activities: Can't resist shooting crumpled papers into trash cans. Runs office pool for every major sporting event and keeps an Excel spreadsheet of staff winnings. Never dawns on him as he's gabbing with his secretary that she has never heard of the San Jose Sharks, much less who plays backup goalie for them.

My Advice: This guy was usually a first-stringer on my team, but if he fumbled the ol' project pigskin before dribbling it across the client's home plate, I brought in another quarterback from the bullpen.

MOTHER (Goose)

Personality: A hugger. Condescending. Saintly.

Appearance: Wears crocheted sweater atop substantial bosom. Uses too much perfume.

Activities: Brings in cookies every Monday. Keeps handy an extensive supply of greeting cards for every occasion, especially funerals. Has a drawer in which she is able, by careful and precise organization, to store two railroad cars worth of condiments, antacids, swabs, buttons, and every other conceivable item anyone might ever think they need. Stays late after work to dust areas the cleaning crew overlooks.

My Advice: She saved me from embarrassment more than once on the way to meet clients by noticing bits of food on my chin, lipstick on my cheek, or bed feathers on my suit. She warmed to Nicholas immediately and was constantly trying to cheer him up.

FLIRT (Peacock)

Personality: Says "Good morning," and pretends not to mean anything by it.

Appearance: Any attractive female.

Activities: Becomes alert when powerful people like me enter the room, then tries to make herself scarce. Grows nervous when we sit down next to her and begin complimenting her figure, clothing, or hairstyle.

My Advice: Every attractive woman in the office flirted with me at one time or another, so it's difficult for me to explain how to avoid this if you don't care for it.

BUBBLY (Chipmunk)

Personality: Always smiling. Perky. Head in the clouds.

Appearance: Wears bright, flowery clothing. White teeth. Drives a pink VW Beetle.

Activities: Always in an upbeat mood and expects everyone else to join in.

My Advice: I fired one of these syrup dispensers once for no reason other than to see if I could wipe that smile off her face. Before she left she thanked me for the opportunity, teeth beaming, and presented me with a gift. I ended up rehiring her simply as an excuse to return the gift. (It was some sort of music box with a baby Elvis atop a fairy horse that sang "Love Me Tender" in a chipmunk voice.)

EXCUSES (Donkey)

Personality: Annoying.

Appearance: Slovenly, unkempt. Clothes often don't match. Car averages one flat per month, and her kids are constantly fighting an infection.

Activities: This individual is often late and performs substandard work. Of course, she has an excuse every time. A favorite line: "I'm sorry, Mr. Ablebright, but the computer deleted that file." She seldom makes it to after-hour employee functions, which is just as well.

My Advice: I kept at least one of these around simply to infuriate Snarler Pit Bulls.

EARLY RETIREE (Panda)

Personality: Easy-going and carefree. A bit inexact on details unless it's his 401(k).

Appearance: Wears soft-soled shoes and the occasional golf visor. Has permanent indentation in right shoulder from leaning against doorposts. Constantly whistling "Copacabana" or "The Banana Song."

Activities: This guy is still two years away from retirement but has basically cashed it in. All he talks about on coffee breaks is the Virgin Islands. He's out the door ten minutes early every day (frequently with a moving box in hand) and is known to extend his lunches to break up the dull routine of rearranging his office furniture.

My Advice: Panda is a bad influence on a generation like yours that openly entertains fantasies of retiring within ten years of one's hiring date. Stay away from him.

HYPOCHONDRIAC (Guinea Pig)
Personality: Sickly. Listless. Feels neglected.

Appearance: Either overweight or thin as a fence post. Worry lines on forehead. Wears expression of suffering.

Activities: Claims to have contracted a variety of illnesses, including a virus from her computer. Has tried every drug and treatment known to medical science, so now resorts to home remedies and medieval concoctions found on the Internet. Frequently goes home early.

My Advice: I can't relate to these types. I didn't use a sick day in forty years—in fact, I even came in with chicken pox once. That's the kind of dedication she can't fathom. I generally avoid her like the plague, but if I could clean out the competition like she can clean out her colon, we'd dominate the industry.

PINBALL (Salmon)
Personality: Fatalistic. Tries to go with the flow. Proud graduate of the school of hard knocks.

Appearance: Slightly purplish, bruised features. Takes mass transit to work.

Activities: Always seems to be in the middle of the latest company crisis. Gets transferred a lot. Has a knack for being in the wrong place at the wrong time.

My Advice: I used these Weebles as punching bags without feeling guilty about it. In fact, they almost seemed to enjoy it. It would be fun to take one to Pamplona for the "Running of the Bulls."

HANDWRINGER (Chihuahua)
Personality: Anxious. Fidgety.

Appearance: Large, serious eyes. Thinning hair. Pale.

Activities: This poor soul is the first to hear of storms that are still days away and will eye the package delivery guy suspiciously for signs of a hidden grenade launcher. Every assignment is considered impossible at the start and a miracle upon completion. I had one secretary who was so troubled by chaos theory that she regularly stifled sneezes for fear they'd ultimately lead to a deadly hurricane forming in the tropics.

My Advice: I never let these types answer the phone—their nervous voices would have been enough to convince the caller to immediately hang up and dial the police SWAT team.

OBLIVIOUS (Olive)

Personality: Head in clouds. Blissfully unaware. Stares for hours at ordinary items like rug stains and cigarette smoke.

Appearance: Vacant or daffy expression. Forgets to zip and button clothes. Piece of apple from lunch stuck to lip all afternoon. Can't remember where her car is parked—or even whether she shut it off.

Activities: Is oblivious that 1) she has left parts of fifteen lunches in the office refrigerator, 2) the turbine-like fan she has in her cubicle blows everyone's papers into the jet stream, 3) she runs over and injures at least three employees a day with the mail cart. In her wake are jammed copier machines, clients left on hold for days, and vault doors left wide open. When she remembers her password and can get on her computer, she opens every email attachment—no matter how inane—and infects the company's network with the latest viruses.

My Advice: This person is so unaware of what's going on around her that I took her nickname from a plant rather than an animal. Every work assignment had to be explained over and over, and she still had no idea what I wanted. She couldn't understand why I fired her, but it didn't matter because she showed up for work the next day anyway, and I had to fire her all over again.

KINDERGARTNER (Fawn)

Personality: Helpless.

Appearance: Large, helpless eyes. Frequently locks self out of car.

Activities: She has to be shown a hundred times how to use the copier and the microwave, and she still confuses the two. Responds to every directive with a question. Manager: "Can you print this for me?" Fawn: "Print it?" Manager: "Yes—it won't take long." Fawn: "It won't?"

My Advice: Whether she was really this helpless was open to debate, but we kept her around because she made the rest of us look like geniuses.

EAGER (Beaver)

Personality: Naïve. Optimistic. Boundless energy. So enthusiastic it's painful for others to watch.

Appearance: Well-dressed in the morning, but disheveled by afternoon due to a furious work pace. Often goes cross-town to pick up gourmet lunches for everyone in the office. Jogs to and from work, even in blizzards.

Activities: Fresh out of school, a young greenhorn is ignorant about the complexities of office politics. Left on his own, he would probably spill his life story to both the Gadabout Parrot and Backstabber Snake before lunch on his first day. He'd fall in love with Flirt Peacock at first sight, initiate pulmonary resuscitation on Hypochondriac Guinea Pig, kneel at the foot of Know-It-All Owl, pledge lifelong adoration of Mother Goose, swallow every syllable Exaggerator Rooster offers, make pathetic overtures toward Nonconformist Cat and Too Quiet Termite, laugh at all of Clown Otter's antics, empathize with Complainer Crow until even he couldn't stand any more, and apologize a dozen times to Easily Offended Horse—all by the end of the first week.

My Advice: Because some of us executives have become bigger than rock stars, I've had a few of these easily impressed tadpoles faint at the mere mention of my name and position. However, these types have gradually become less common.

N: *Labeling*

Apparently, my generation of tadpoles is not as prone to fainting as previous ones.

　　Hub found it humorous as he showed me around the office to whisper to me each individual's type. But what was much funnier was when I learned that one person he had identified as a Flirt Peacock (with the hots for Hub, naturally) was actually a lesbian (yet another label!).

H: *Survival Of The Fittest*

A lesbian? When did that happen? She was fine two months ago. I can see I'm going to have to invent a new category.

Even though I know most of you have only seen wild animals on television, I have given each employee type an animal designation to make it easier to characterize and remember them, and also to reinforce the point that, just as in nature, a kind of "survival of the fittest" mechanism occurs over time. Left to itself, this mechanism will eliminate the weaker types (identified in the lower half of the list) and leave only the strongest. This is bad news for you as you rise through the managerial ranks, for they will invariably turn their attention toward fighting *you*. As Swift once wrote, "When a true genius appears in the world, you may know him by this sign, that the dunces are all in confederacy against him."

Your strategy then must be to keep the strongest divided and preoccupied trying to eliminate the weaker ones. You do this by actively undercutting the strong and playing them against each other. All along you continually prop up the weak, always taking their side. Not only will this gain you fame as a champion of the oppressed, it will force the strong to keep their eyes on who's reaching up from below rather than on who sits above.

N: *Turf Battles*

End turf battles by ripping up the turf. Bickering and office politicking usually need a long-term environment to develop. That's why I'm a big believer in fewer long-term business relationships. I can see a day when people will become commodities or entities who go from project to project, rarely staying in the same place for long. The walls of companies will become much more fluid, like an amoeba.

H: *Maintaining Your Cast Of Characters*

An amoeba? Where does he come up with this stuff? First we had the "new" economy—next it will be the "protozoan" economy.

Companies as we know them have been around a long, long time, and that's not going to change any time soon. Therefore, it is important to maintain a full stable of the various characters described in this chapter if you want to ensure a balance between weak and strong personalities in your company.

5

IMAGE

H: *Image Is . . .*

I met up with Nicholas one day after he had left the company. I was walking the short distance from my parking space to the main building when I noticed him. His sweaty face was soiled with dirt, and he was pushing a squeaky wheelbarrow.

"Nicholas—what a surprise! I see you've latched on with our landscaping contractor."

"Yeah. Just something until I get my studio going."

"And, in the meantime a little dirt won't hurt—even if it was one of your ilk who said, 'Image is everything.'"

"Corporate jingles don't speak for me."

"Well, then, on that we agree. Image has never meant anything to me, either."

"Okay, *Dr.* Ablebright."

"I only used that title because that particular audience needed reassurance."

Like Ramses, I then left Moses to his mud and straw and hurried in to meet an important client in the mahogany conference room—no place for Nicholas now, but one in which he had not so long ago comfortably reclined. What I'd told him just then about "image" was true. It's not the parsley that makes a great steak.

N: *What Is It With Lawns?*

Did you ever notice the older generations' obsession with lawn care? Once my parents moved to that new subdivision, it was nitpick city. I swear some of our neighbors were out there with stimp meters after they cut their grass. And, if you let an extra day go by without cutting your lawn, you could feel the glaring eyes from the judge and jury searing into you as you shot hoops out in the driveway. Then, Mrs. Crabgrass would set aside her garden prong and wander over under some pretense so she could lift her bifocals and get a close-up look at the offending yard that was lowering property values all over a ten-block area.

I mention this because corporate campuses have the same obsession. Is there some kind of law that says every suburban office building must be surrounded by ten acres of mowed lawn? It makes no sense. Spend money fertilizing and watering grass to make it grow so you have to cut it—then water it again so it grows again so you have to cut it again. The foreman on the landscaping crew told me lawn grasses aren't the best at soaking up rainwater, so then all of these retention ponds have to be built. He said native grasses do a better job and they require less maintenance.

Someone in my parents' subdivision tried a natural lawn once. I guess that didn't portray the right image. The neighbors called the weed commissioner (that's not what you think) and he burned it out while the owners were on vacation.

H: *Personal Names*

Landscaping aside, I personally paid little attention to appearances, striving instead for substance in all aspects of my life. When I aimed for consistency I found that image took care of itself. Simply be true to yourself and make no apologies for it. That said, I have included in this chapter a few ways to enhance the self you are being true to.

Whose songs would you rather listen to, Henry John Deutchendorf's or John Denver's? Who was more likely to play a leading man in Hollywood, Archie Leach or Cary Grant? Both of these individuals changed their names early in their careers, and undoubtedly their decisions played a role in their later successes.

What about you? Unless you're named Harry Crack, changing your name is probably a bit drastic, especially if you're Old Money. The best strategy, then, is to maximize what you already have. Play around with different combinations. One of my old business partners, for example, could legitimately be known as Sir Dr. Wilbert Henry Benson, Jr. III, Esq., but he settled for Sir Henry Benson, Esq. several years ago because it was easier to sign autographs.

Most people have nicknames or middle names they can substitute for first names. They usually have titles they can add or subtract, initials they can use, distinguished maternal names they can add with a hyphen, and so forth. Find a name you're comfortable with and give it a chance. If your career takes off, stay with it. If opportunities slow to a crawl, it may be time to tinker.

N: *Single Names*

I used to be named I. Q. Weighhigh, but I felt too self-conscious, so I changed it to something more ordinary.

I wonder what Hub would think of single monikers like Prince or Bono? I can probably guess. Maybe they'd be acceptable if they were Prince IV or Dr. Bono.

H: *Company Names*

I once owned a Doberman named Prince. "Here, Prince, fetch the Bono."

Someday, if you're very lucky, you may have the opportunity to spin off your own company or be instrumental in the renaming of a new company following a merger. Just how important is a company name? Aren't management, marketing, and quality products and services what determine success or failure? You're damn right.

Yet, you'd never know it in this upside down era where branding and image are the cat's meow. The way things are going we'll soon see companies springing up with drug-induced, oddball names like FatBrain or Loudcloud. How did we get to this point?

It all began when revered, established companies that should have known better chose to simply become known by their initials. Neglecting its rich history, International Business Machines became IBM. (I don't know about you, but that makes me think of missiles.) American Telephone & Telegraph abandoned its glorious moniker for the meaningless acronym AT&T (sounds like a grocery store). Others made the move for reasons of "political correctness." Fried foods were getting a bad rap, so now we have KFC.

Companies like Exxon initiated the next step in this sad decline by using non-word names. The trend has picked up steam, marked by the coming-out parties for Agilent, Sitara, and Adero, along with dozens of others. One magazine featured a quiz that asked respondents to separate recent company names from pharmaceuticals, and I'm guessing plenty of people will mistakenly phone in orders for Agilent the next time their hayfever acts up. The goal of the names, apparently, is to convey a high-tech image, and to avoid the baggage that might follow more common words. (I get a good laugh when some of these techie names end up meaning something unflattering in a foreign language like Mexican.)

There's nothing wrong with a tried-and-true name like Smith & Sons. In the old days, personal reputations meant something, so folks were proud to put their names on their letterhead. And people knew exactly what they did for a living. You sold auto parts and you did it at honest prices, so you called yourself Trusty Auto. Today, nobody can describe what the hell he does anymore in a single sentence that makes sense. Is it any surprise that people hide behind ridiculous job titles and meaningless corporate banners?

N: *New Name*

A bunch of us office rats were sitting in a booth down at the watering hole having a couple of beers after work. Naturally, the discussion turned to one of our favorite subjects—how we could get the Hubster to flip his lid.

"Wouldn't it be great if we got together and bought him out?" Derek said, edging forward on his seat.

"Of course we'd keep him as a figurehead," said Janelle, who was always thinking ahead.

I ordered another brew, and then said, "We'd make his office a little kid's desk in the hallway."

"And we'd change the name of the company," Derek said enthusiastically.

"To what?"

"Something he'd just hate."

"Like?"

We all thought for a moment. Then Derek, perhaps noticing Janelle's diamond stud, offered, "How about Diamondeaters Solutions, Inc. Definitely cutting edge."

"Not bad," Janelle said, "but I think he'd prefer something like ButterHornet Corporation, a company that blends the mean independence of the hornet with the soft, bonding qualities of butter."

"Who could resist that kind of synergy?" I said.

"I think that's already taken," Serena, a new hire in accounting, said, rolling her eyes at the three of us.

"What I want to know is, how does Yodaco fit in?" I said. "Hub claims it's some sort of partner company, but you never see or hear of anyone who works there."

"Yodaco. . . ." repeated Serena. "Why does that sound familiar?"

H: *Professional Attire*

I fear for the future of my grandson. For now, at least, he remains innocent. He has a little joke he likes to repeat to me:

"What did the shoes say to the hat? You go on ahead—I'll catch up when I get back on my feet."

I'll have to remember that one for Brittany (my new wife). That's about her speed. I'll probably have to explain the "ahead" part though.

I'm not going to tell you where to put your hat or your shoes. Undoubtedly, you will be ridiculously overdressed or embarrassingly underdressed on your first day anyway. You can then see for yourself what is appropriate at your workplace and adjust accordingly. There were, however, questions I received from new hires now and then.

- **Question:** "I've noticed our CEO wearing sandals, golf shoes, and slippers with his suits—may I?"
  Answer: The CEO can go barefoot if he chooses. Not only should you avoid doing the same, you should not even notice what the CEO wears or doesn't wear.

- **Q:** "How long should my socks be?"
  A: Wear short socks under your slacks to ensure the hair on your shins is exposed when you put your feet up on your desk. (Let your staff say what they will about you—at least there'll be no whispers that you shave your legs.)

- **Q:** "Should I dress up for certain clients?"
  A: Don't dress for your clients—dress for your clients' secretaries.

- **Q:** "Is a tie always necessary?"
  A: Wearing a dress shirt buttoned at the collar but minus a tie may look "chic" to some, but to me it says you either don't know how to tie a tie, or your clip-on is in the wash.

- **Q:** "I'm a big fan of 'dress down' days. Have you considered expanding your 'casual Friday' policy to the entire week?"
  A: Who said we had a "casual Friday" policy? If you really want casual days, you can stay in your pajamas all week while you're *unemployed*.

- **Q:** "Will people accept me if I show up at the next board meeting with an earring?"
  A1: Sure—but you should probably insist that your secretary wear a bit more than that.
  A2: Trying this stunt at *my* board meeting would have gotten you a ring for your neck.

- **Q:** "I'd like to show off the tattoos on my arms, but wearing a suit and long sleeve shirt all day makes that impossible. Any suggestions?"
  A: Remove the sleeves from the shirts you wear to work. Wait for a day when the air conditioning breaks down at the office and remove your jacket. (Why do I have to think of everything?)

- **Q:** "Do you think hats will ever come back in fashion?"
  A: I always hoped so. I kept several hanging on the rack next to my Tommy gun.

N: *Grooming*

You don't need Hub and me to teach you how to floss properly. (That's

Mother Goose's job!) Nevertheless, it's easy to miss something, and since Hub repeatedly told me that one grooming misstep can undo years of stellar performance, I'd better share some insights.

- Ear, nose, and neck hair is frowned upon when you are younger but looks distinguished when you get older.

- Do not cover shaving cuts with small bits of toilet paper. Inevitably you will forget to remove the bloodstained paper from your face until around lunchtime.

- If, like Hub, you awaken from an afternoon catnap with "bed head," it is best to slip on a golf visor and leave for the course immediately.

- A shot of peppermint schnapps wards off bad breath better than gum or mouthwash.

- Don't wait until hair loss is out of control. Get fitted for that toupee before anyone will notice.

- If dandruff shows when you wear black, and dirt shows when you wear white, wear gray or polka dots.

- If you run out of Old Spice cologne, you can swipe an extra bottle out of Harry Baxter's desk drawer when he's out to lunch with the other VPs.

H: *Plastic Surgery*

Finally, some decent advice from that tenderfoot.

Even though there's no reason your contemporaries should be worried about their looks already, I've noticed plenty of young people hanging around the local cosmetology office. Some even go so far as to inject a paralyzing substance called Botox into the skin on their faces. Apparently, they've also been injecting *Botox* into their *buttocks*, because I've seen plenty of dead asses lately.

Using surgery to remove forehead lines, double chins, sagging jowls, and crow's feet is perfectly acceptable. Admitting to it is not. There are multiple strategies you can use.

1) Go away for a while.

"Well, Mr. Smith, that long vacation certainly looks to have refreshed you."

"Thank you. My features have always responded well to salt water and the tropical air."

2) Grow a thick beard about a month before the surgery.
"My, you look so different, Mr. Smith."
"Ah, you're not used to me without the beard."

3) Provide a reasonable explanation.
"Mr. Smith, did you. . . ?"
"Quit smoking cigars? You bet I did. Amazing the difference it's made."

N: *Fountain Of Youth*

Hub liked to point out on a regular basis how young he thought he looked: "Had another high school reunion last weekend. Saints alive! I might have aged a little and added a few extra pounds, but you should have seen everyone else! I couldn't figure out if I was at an old folks home or a hog roast."

"Britney keeps you young," I offered.

"If I dyed my hair I'd look 55, easy."

"No doubt," I agreed.

"And if I took off a little weight, I wouldn't look a day over 50."

And if he put a bag over his head, he could pass for 40.

H: *Cell Phones*

I hate to say it, but *you're* the ones who look silly. Young people can't even get out of the company parking lot and they've already got a phone glued to their ears. Whenever I strolled through the break room or past the benches outside, I'd see everyone sitting off on their own, in the middle of another call.

Seminars let out, and, while the execs head for cocktails, all of the young lemmings stream out into the corridors. Within milliseconds, they have their phones stuck to their ears. Then, droning with useless conversation, they pace back and forth, putting one foot slowly in front of the other in some kind of trance-like parade.

Even more pathetic is the content of these "incredibly important" phone calls, snippets of which I have reproduced on the next page.

Lemming 1: "Heather, did I get any calls?" (Heaven forbid that you couldn't get back to somebody until tomorrow!)

Lemming 2: "Yeah, another session just ended. I'm out in the hallway now." (Where will he be next? Watch for a follow-up on *World News Tonight*.)

Lemming 3: "Is this Jeremy? Oh—Trina. He must have given me the wrong digits. So . . . what's up with you?" (The main thing is you're on the phone—who cares who answers, right?)

Lemming 4: "What's the latest? Is Cisco still in free fall? How about the NASDAQ?" (You wouldn't have to worry about it if you were in for the long haul like you're supposed to be.)

Lemming 5: "No, I can't skip out early to go kite surfing. My frickin' boss is here." (And, he's frickin' watching you like a frickin' hawk.)

Lemming 6: "Where are you?!" (Probably three feet away, on a different cell phone.) "I need your laptop—mine keeps locking up when I hook the projector to it." (Ever seen overhead transparencies lock up? Didn't think so.)

Lemming 7: "Hey, can you still hear me?. . . How about now?" (Try again in another hour—I'm sure they'll have another one of those monstrous cell towers up by then.)

If you are so enchained by popular culture that you feel you must carry a cell phone, at least refrain from giving out your phone number. Only greenhorns think getting a call is a status symbol. It's far better to give the impression that you are *too important* to be interrupted with calls.

N: *Well-Kept Secret*
There's another reason not to give out your phone number. The higher up the management ladder you go, the less you probably want to be found.

6

NETWORKING

H: _Real Networking_

Sorry to disappoint you, but sitting up all night in a chat room is _not_ considered legitimate business networking. Idle gossip is vastly different from the purposeful communication I intend to discuss here.

"Working the room" and "pressing the flesh" are more important these days than ever before. Fed a steady, bland diet of phone conferences, video meetings, and online seminars, people crave honest-to-goodness personal contact. But it takes a well-rounded, well-read individual to keep a conversation going with a variety of folks. Unfortunately, this background is precisely the opposite of what today's graduates receive from increasingly specialized university-degree programs. Politics, history, geography, and other basics of a solid education—topics that can become important tools for casual business conversation—are all neglected. Study after study shows most students are so specialized that they fall on their faces when asked who the vice president is or where Europe is located on a map.

N: *They're Still Falling For It*

It cracks me up when I see a terminally serious "think tank" guy with knit brows and a scrunched up forehead bemoaning the "sorry state" of the American education system. Then, he cites statistics showing how 20 percent of college students couldn't identify the vice president and 35 percent confused Africa with South America on a map. Don't these researchers know how much college students like to screw around on these stupid "tests"? When I was in school, a bunch of us would see who could come up with the most ridiculous answer. One guy wrote down "Howard Stern" as the VP. (Like it really matters anyway who the vice president is.)

H: *The True Difference Maker*

I would have expected more from a generation that constantly yearns to be judged on merit. Nicholas, for example, wanted to believe that his creativity, his ability to innovate, the power of his solutions, and the energy of his efforts would be properly recognized and rewarded. Wrong. If Nicholas had stuck around a little longer, he would have come to realize that it's the back-slapping, hand-shaking fellow—the one who copies other people's ideas, takes credit for their solutions, and spends more time golfing than working—who gets the promotions and the big raises.

How does the fellow of supposedly lesser ability do it? Networking. It really does come down to *who* you know, not *what* you know. I realize that's a tough pill for you to swallow. But, the fact is, the technically illiterate guy who hobnobs with top executives at Microsoft will get farther in the computer industry than the greatest programmer in the world.

Finally ready for a few lessons in networking? And, even though you now know I'm not talking about cables and servers, I'm going to show you how nice I really am. I'm going to put this lesson in terms you'll be able to relate to.

H: *The Fundamentals*

I had Nicholas jot down for me all of the computer networking terms he could think of. Guess what? There really are links between working the crowd and stringing cable.

1) **"Redundancy" is a good thing**.
   Don't limit yourself to phone calls. Send notes. Meet in person. Reserve a campsite next to his on your next vacation.
   > "Hi, again! I just came over to borrow some marsh-mallows. While I'm here . . ."

2) **"Ping" to verify somebody's home**.
   Before you waste time, make sure there's somebody at the other end who is worth your efforts. There's nothing worse than gaining a commitment from somebody who has no power to make it binding.
   > "Who did you say you were?" you ask again.
   > "Clem. I'm in charge of the wetvac."

3) **"Always on" is the most useful connection**.
   Your benefactor or potential client is not like a server—he can't process hundreds of communications at once. There's only one pathway. Consequently, when you're conversing on the phone with him, nobody else can communicate with him but you. The instant you cease communications, somebody else—a competitor maybe—can occupy that narrow band-width. Clearly, it's important that you stay connected until you get what you want. Similar to a real network line, *what* you send isn't important. Therefore, "data" consisting of flattery, while not as effective as a sincere compliment, is still useful because it keeps your connection alive.
   > "Well, I really need to go now," he'll probably say. "The security guard just turned out the lights."
   > "I really like your openness! Say, why don't you give me your cell number and I'll give you those quotes again."

4) **Nobody likes it when everything is "down."**
   This is true not only for computer networks but also for people-to-people networking. It's important to keep your interaction positive. Other people like to be around people who are optimistic, not negative all the time. This is a tough one for your melancholy generation. I once saw a greeting card on the divider in Nicholas' work area that read:

   > *All I know is the beat goes on and on*
   > *And will be the same, 'til the day I'm gone.*

Nobody loves me!! Nobody cares.
Maybe I'll go eat worms. – Limp Bizkit

I'd be limp too if I went around humming that all day. Older generations are a lot more positive, and you can see it in their song lyrics. I remember sending a card to my first wife that paraphrased this uplifting ditty from Tom Jones:

Well you're never in the way
Something always nice to say, Oh what a blessing.
I can leave you on your own
Knowing you're okay alone, and there's no messing.

Go back a few years earlier and you can see even more positive themes running through song lyrics, such as this one sung by cheerful crooner Tony Bennett:

I know I'd go from rags to riches
If you would only say you care
And though my pocket may be empty
I'd be a millionaire.

Now there's a "look on the bright side," attitude. I'd hire somebody with an outlook like that in a New York minute.

5) Effective connections require the proper "protocol" and "handshake."
I don't understand exactly how the terms "protocol" and "handshake" fit in with computer networking, but I heard them bandied about by techies outside my office. However, I do know how they relate to interpersonal relations. Polite greetings and firm handshakes are essential. So is knowing how to properly slap a back (you do it with your hand *cupped* so you don't knock the wind out of the other fellow).

Although a little formality wouldn't hurt, standards have relaxed a bit over the years. You needn't wait for someone like Ed McMahon to introduce you before you can speak to someone you don't know. Nor do you have to be announced at the door. Conference and office get-togethers are not the Howell's Cotillion—it's okay to butt in and start handing out your business cards.

6) Work with superior, quality "equipment."

Spending all of your evening networking with losers is a waste of time. You need to learn how to spot important people. Below are several clues that somebody is worth pursuing.

- **Age:** At the very least they are older than you are. Even better if they look over 50.

- **Name tag:** The most important people never need to wear one.

- **Shoes, clothing:** They don't look like they dressed themselves.

- **Crowd:** They're never alone, not even for a moment. The people surrounding them laugh or smile at *everything* they say.

- **Attendants:** Various assistants carry their briefcases, wallets, and golf clubs.

- **Awareness:** If they notice an entry-level professional like you or introduce themselves to you, they are not that important.

- **Women:** The females in their entourage are gorgeous. (They don't notice you either.)

N: *Conversation Topics*

Okay, now that we've been schooled by an expert, it's time to get out on the floor. We've been told our skills and talents aren't going to get us anywhere. Therefore, we can't afford to be seen leaning against the wall by ourselves looking like we ought to be shipped back to the Island of Misfit Toys. Don't be intimidated by professionals who are older than you are. Go up to a group of executives and start rappin'.

> *Tha word on the street come loud and clear*
> *You think you tha lead but you bringin up tha rear.*
> *Wearin yo spectacles—backwardz. (Who me?)*
> *Ridin yo bicycles—backwardz. (Yeah, you!)*
> *Can't see past yo self-impo'tence*

Fo'get who makes all yo appo'ntments.
Showin yo momma them Gs on yo money tree
You and integrity mix like Shaq and a referee.

If rappin's not your scene, the next best thing is to have a couple of topics prepared ahead of time. Just make sure you keep the conversation locked on *them*, or they will quickly lose interest. Beware of committing the unpardonable sin of discussing a topic outside their rigidly defined interests or values. The following are proven conversation starters I've heard and guaranteed conversation killers blurted out by people who weren't thinking.

Your Starter: "Who's the greatest golfer of all time?"
Exec 1: "Well, Slammin' Sammy Snead had eighty-one tour victories. Watching him practice golf was like watching a fish practice swimming."
Exec 2: "But the Golden Bear won something like eighteen majors. What an athlete."
Killer: "Don't you think Tiger Woods could whip any of those old players?"

Your Starter: "How do you like that sexpot in the green dress?"
Exec 1: "Whoa, baby! Backfield in motion! Hut, hut!"
Exec 2: "She can't be older than 25, 26. Let's see, I'm 56—that's just right."
Killer: "Yeah, we're tight. She's takin' me to a rave tomorrow night."

Your Starter: "Say, did you ever try a raw egg in your beer?"
Exec 1: "All the time, and we never got sick."
Exec 2: "An oyster is pretty good too."
Killer: "You know what's even better—a lime in a Corona."

Your Starter: "My boss is looking for a name for our new corporate jet—any suggestions?"
Exec 1: "How about the *Silver Eagle*?"
Exec 2: "I like *Seraphim*."
Killer: "I was kind of thinking *Vulture*. You know, circles for a while, picks everything clean, then moves on."

Your Starter: "Any of you know how to set up your severance agreement so you get more if you are forced out than if you serve out your full contract?"
Exec 1: "Great idea! And they say we've lost our ability to innovate."
Exec 2: "I can give you some names to contact."

Killer: "Oh, it's for my boss. I personally think that kind of thing is unethical."

Your Starter: "That Democrat Traficant sure is an odd duck, isn't he?"
Exec 1: "Ohio has an official state bird, an official state reptile, and an official state idiot—and that guy is all three."
Exec 2: "Did you see who voted to keep him? Condit! Thank God I'm a Republican."
Killer: "I'm kind of leaning toward the Green Party myself."

N: *The Art Of Interrupting*

Usually you will find that conversations don't need starting. Long-winded VIPs are already talking (often quoting themselves), and what you need to do is find a way to hack into the conversation. Just standing there and listening won't accomplish anything, because afterward the participants in the discussion will only think to themselves, "That young man who joined our group listened and nodded pleasantly enough. I wonder who he was?" That doesn't do you a whole lot of good in the long run.

You need to break in. You could stand there and wait politely for a pause—which should come about the year 2015—or you could grab control immediately with these "hooks," which are guaranteed to stop cold whatever discussion a group is having and yank it in a completely different direction.

- "I clicked on your company Web site, and it went straight to a porn page."

- "After what I heard at the board meeting yesterday, I know why the SEC considers insider trading illegal!"

- "So, you guys are in plastics. I heard that organic plastics start-up just got its first big contract. Isn't that something how their stuff breaks down naturally?"

- "Hey, I just heard another big accounting firm got busted. I bet you all would like to know which one."

- "Did you see the research that suggests the brains of younger people are more highly evolved because they've grown up using their thumbs more?"

- "Some reporter stopped by yesterday looking for info about a company named Yodaco. Any of you guys know anything?"

H: *Getting Rid Of Somebody*

I have often faced a problem that is just the opposite of the previous one. I have been imprisoned in conversations from which there seemed to be no ready escape.

Forget swimming—this is where the buddy system really proves its worth. Over the years my various "buddies" and I perfected a series of signals to let each other know when we were in trouble. Years ago, before we had figured out the complexities of what we were doing, we used to try signals such as putting our hands in our back pockets or readjusting our belts. These signals failed miserably in a crowded room because they were usually too difficult to see. Eventually we found that signals such as straightening our ties or patting the tops of our heads were far more effective.

Once the signal is detected, along comes your buddy to interrupt the offending party with an announcement that you are needed immediately on a delicate matter across the room.

N: *Better Have A Backup*

When I figured out that Hub was using this buddy system, I recruited blockers to prevent his buddy from getting through. You should have seen Hub standing there furiously patting his head, wondering where his rescuer was!

H: *The Sound Of A Name*

Dale Carnegie taught that, "A man's name is, to him, the sweetest and most important sound in any language." This is a valuable tip to keep in mind when networking. I, Henry Ablebright, always take extra care to repeat my name—Henry Ablebright—as many times as possible when I, Henry Ablebright, am talking to others. I admit, the sound of my name, Henry Ablebright, *is* very satisfying. And there's no doubt my listeners will remember my name, Henry Ablebright, the next time we meet.

7

OFFICE DÉCOR

H: *A Woman's Touch*

My first wife, Millicent, felt it was her God-given duty to supervise the design of my office. I can still hear her shrill voice as she strutted about like a chicken:

"No, that's *not* the leather chair I ordered. You can't expect him to sit on *that*. And don't lose those pictures. I want the one of the children right there on his desk. Yes, right there, next to the 'Buck Stops Here' sign. Then put the large one of Hub and me so it can be seen immediately when people walk in. Who put this other picture of me in the waste paper basket? I told you I wanted this one on the wall behind his chair. Right above it. Now take that one of the whole family and put it on the conference table with the rest of the centerpiece."

N: *All For Nothing*

Try as she might to keep a watchful eye on her husband in her absence, Millicent's picture above Hub's chair was as clueless as she was.

H: *Guiding Principles Of Design*

Office décor needs to accomplish three things: 1) provide for your personal comfort, 2) get unessential visitors out of your domain as soon as possible, and, when the time comes, 3) verify your position of power.

N: *Furnishings*

"It looks like a feed mill around here. I hope you disinfected that stuff," Hub snorted, as he inspected the area around my cubicle.

"I made some great finds at the flea market," I said. "Do you like how I turned that old crate into a bookshelf?"

"Charming. Didn't you see the nice globes in the last catalog?"

"I don't really need one of those."

"Well, you ought to have something snazzy around here."

"Snazzy?"

"You know, decorative."

"I saw some stuff at Target that I might get."

"Oh, really? I've never been in there."

H: *Open-Door Policy*

Time was when executive offices were strictly off-limits to all but the most privileged. Then along came the era of "sensitive management" and feel-good attempts to empower employees by encouraging easy access and unending listening sessions. Suddenly every common staffer in the place was setting up accommodations in executive office suites and bleating their tales of woe to sympathetic, nodding executives. Execs became therapists instead of the high-powered deal brokers they were hired to be. Not unexpectedly, productivity declined, and profits headed south.

Pandora's box has been opened, and there is probably no return. What has been so cavalierly given away will simply not be wrested back. Fortunately, in times of crisis one's resourcefulness rises to the challenge. Over the years I perfected a variety of techniques that kept up the appearance of an "open-door" policy while effectively discouraging any such thing. There may not be a whole lot of privacy among your generation, but mine had well-defined limits that I aimed to enforce.

I always made it a point to smile at the end of the perfunctory introductions, when new staffers are brought around, and say with all the warmth of a cheap greeting card, "My door is always open, so stop by any time you have concerns." Not in my wildest imagination did I mean this, of course, but this clear statement kept them off balance later when doubts threatened to enter.

Let's dream a bit and pretend you're upper management for a moment. You're cornered in your private office by a sad sack who's been slumped over your desk for what seems like an eternity, mumbling something about feeling unfulfilled in his current career track. Or, maybe it's some manager's secretary perched across from you and complaining about an incidental pat on her behind. How do you limit these intrusions?

- **Keep your office door *wide open*.** Your visitor will glance anxiously at the passing foot traffic and may even ask you to close the door. This is where you firmly repeat your "My door is *always* open" speech and warmly add, "We have no secrets here." Believe me, this will keep the conversation from getting too personal.

- **Maintain a chilly office temperature to discourage visitors from staying too long.** For your own comfort, use a space heater under your desk or position your chair so that the sunshine coming through the window keeps you toasty.

- **Purchase chairs with rollers, then have maintenance saw down the back two legs about a half inch.** Any visitor sitting in such a chair will ever so slowly roll backward toward the door. In five minutes they'll be out in the hallway, right where you want them.

- **Keep your clock set five to seven minutes ahead.** This will make it seem later than it actually is, which has two advantages: 1) people will immediately feel indebted to you for excusing their tardiness, and 2) appointments will end that much sooner, so you can get back to reading *Barron's*.

- **Instruct your secretary beforehand to ring your telephone about ten minutes into the meeting.**

Carry on a brief conversation with yourself, speaking lines such as, "No, I'll have to call you back as soon as I get done here. Yes, I promise. Just as soon as I get done. I'll try, but I don't know how much longer this will go."

N: *Not What You Think*

"Hey, Mr. Ablebright, I thought you had an open-door policy," I said to Hub on his way out one evening.

"Why, I most certainly do."

"That's not what I hear from that new intern."

"There's a perfectly reasonable explanation. *She* closed the door, not me. Nicholas, you come back here—and wipe that smile off your face!"

H: *Judging A Book By Its Cover*

Like it or not, we all make surface judgments every day (especially Nicholas). For instance, no one can read each book before deciding whether to buy it. Knowing, therefore, that people could not "read" me in the short time they had, I made sure my "cover" was impressive. I started by filling my bookshelf with the appropriate titles.

> Books for Display
> *Lives of the Saints*
> *A History of Celibacy*
> *A Higher Standard of Leadership: Lessons from Gandhi*
> *What Great Paintings Say: Masterpieces in Detail*
> *Team Management: Leadership by Consensus*
> *Seven Habits of Highly Effective People*

N: *More Books*

Don't let Hub fool you with the books he displayed (or cooked). I've seen what he really read:

> Books Hub Reads But Keeps Out of Sight
> *William Randolph Hearst: Press Baron*
> *Mantrack: Playboy's Blueprints for Better Living*
> *Loopholes of the Rich: How to Pay Zero Taxes*
> *The Great American Pin-Up (Jumbo Series)*
> *How to Retire Wealthy*
> *Getting What You Want—Now!*

Books Hub Might Write Someday
800-lb. Gorilla Marketing
Leadership Secrets from TV's Sgt. Carter
Diversity: What We Learned from "The Munsters"
Rich Dad, Poor Slob
The Urge to Merge: From the Boardroom to the Bedroom
The Wife of the Millionaire Next Door (Alternate title: *The Derri-ere Next Door*)
Seven Bad Habits I Wish I Could Get More Of

H: *Be Careful Of The Statement You Make*

Some high-minded professionals, who must believe they were Socrates in a former life, like to hang supposedly thought-provoking quotes on their walls. Then I guess we're all expected to bow on our way out. Shortly after Nicholas started, I entered his work area and spotted framed calligraphy that said something like, "Seldom can we handle the storm of truth; it must come upon us drop, by drop, by drop, by drop." Now just what the devil is that supposed to mean?

N: *Come Back From Those Workshops With Something Useful*

Hub told me to attend every workshop and seminar I could that offered a certificate of achievement suitable for framing. Eventually I saw why. Once you obtain enough to cover an entire wall, the effect is far more stunning than calligraphy. Wall space, however, is limited, so sometimes you have to make sacrifices.

"Why did I get this customer appreciation certificate from Private Pleasures Boutique?" I asked Hub one morning after the mail arrived.

"Oh, here, let me put that away," he said, rising quickly from his desk. "I must have used your name by mistake the last time I was in there—a long time ago."

H: *The Inspiration Of Nature*

If you ever hunted or fished, you could have hung a trophy on your wall. It would have been your way of saying, "I took that beast down and I can take you down, too." Since you did all of your hunting in the dark with paintball guns, however, you'll have to find a suitable trophy at one of your flea markets, and invent a story to go with it. If you have qualms about stretching the truth, then you don't deserve to have those deer fangs on your wall. Take the trophy down—you never would have had the guts to shoot it anyway.

One frisky young Ladder Climber Monkey visiting my office fresh off a recent promotion joked that when he passed me by on his climb up the ladder he'd put a dinosaur head on his office wall. By the time he realized what he'd said and who he'd said it to, it was too late. Last I heard he was considerably less frisky, selling used vacuum cleaners door-to-door somewhere north of Saskatchewan.

H: *A Picture Is Worth A Thousand Words*

Since who you know is more important than what you do, you should prominently display photos of yourself with various dignitaries. County fairs and similar events are prime opportunities to obtain a snapshot of you and Senator Bigshot side by side, relaxed and in casual clothing. Also, carry a felt-tip and insist on a signing. In the midst of a lively public setting, he may even add a personal greeting to his name.

Use good judgment though. Visitors to your office might become suspicious if they see a wet-behind-the-ears pollywog like you in photo after photo with incredibly important officials. Use the following chart, which takes into account an employee's status, to guide your photo selections.

YOUR STATUS	PHOTO SUBJECTS	FRAME TYPE
Entry-level professional	City council members	Plastic
Assistant division manager	Mayors and lieutenant governors	Wood
Division manager	State senators and representatives	Pewter
Junior vice president	U.S. senators and representatives	Brass
Senior vice president	State governors	Silver
CFO, COO, etc.	Federal cabinet members and U.S. vice president	Gold
CEO	U.S. president and friendly heads-of-state	Jewel-studded
Chairman of the board	God and Federal Reserve Board chairman	Sorry, no graven mages

N: *Respect Will Come*

Of course, when we rise to the rank of a top-level executive we will no longer have to scour county fairs to make our contacts. Signed photos from elected officials will arrive regularly at our desks in appreciation of our companies' generous campaign contributions.

H: *Executive Restrooms*

Someday this might become important to you. High-ranking managers and executives should have their own private restroom facilities on the managerial or executive wing. We constantly strive to maintain the respect—even awe—of those who depend on us for a living. The activities that occur in a restroom are of such a nature as to be demeaning to all of us. A common staff member sharing the same environment with management may lead to an awkward situation for all involved, especially if the manager is still prone to "stage fright" when addressing the urinal. When I found such an occurrence unavoidable, I simply made a ruse of combing my hair or straightening my tie, and returned after the staffer had left.

N: *Plugged Up*

I can see why Hub would be concerned about restrooms and the impact on executive image. Several of us who occasionally used the restroom on the executive wing began to call one of the stalls the "Hard Rock Café," because there always seemed to be a VP in there struggling to drop a tater in the kettle, so to speak.

8

TECHNOLOGY

H: *Overrated*

I have never needed to use, much less own, a computer. Most veteran executives are careful *not* to become dependent on office technology. Newly hired professionals, weaned on digital this and high-tech that, naturally think they know better. I have news for you: By the time all the software training, corrupt file recoveries, maintenance upgrades, and network downtime is factored in, it's faster to do things the old way.

It's not that I *couldn't* use technology (I could have learned to make copies on the copier as well as the next guy), it's that I *didn't need* to use it. Could Pharaoh have made bricks? More to the point, did he need to?

Furthermore, even when the infernal stuff is working as intended, most technology remains overrated. The facsimile machine, for example, is a tool of dubious value. Take a fresh document, run it through a fax machine, and the poor sap at the other end receives a practically unreadable document that looks like it has been copied 500 times.

"Hi, Hub. Did your secretary send a fax?" came the call.

"Yes, she did. I hope you can decipher it," I typically responded. "Every *c* probably looks like an *o*."

"Actually, I was hoping you could tell me which end of the paper was the top."

N: *Just A Suggestion*
It would probably help if the document to be faxed was produced on a laser printer rather than a mimeograph.

H: *The Information Services ("IS") Department*
At Ablebright Manufacturing, we had no IS ("Internal Sabotage," as I prefer to call it) department. What little support we needed for the few items we had was obtained through a third-party vendor who also took care of our landscaping. Some may view this as an oddity in today's world, but I know from bitter experience what can happen when you create and staff an IS department.

The data processing department at another manufacturing company I helped manage started out small, with a couple of Too Quiet Termite types, a Know-It-All Owl, and a Nonconformist Cat hunched over their keypunch cards in what used to be an old storage closet. This gang pretty much kept to itself for a while, with the only trouble occurring *within* the department (Cat wanted Apple, others wanted IBM, etc.). Despite this inner turmoil a few decent improvements were rolled out and the brass rewarded them with a bigger budget.

That's when an Excuses Donkey and a Handwringer Chihuahua were hired, and the problems really began. Suddenly, the Chihuahua was fretting that "mission critical" applications were dangerously exposed without redundancy systems, firewalls, and secret handshakes. More techies were hired and one of the assembly lines was shut down to make room. The Donkey told the brass that the increasing crashes and glitches were due to obsolete software and hardware. More money was allocated to the burgeoning department, and it changed its name to the Division of Information Services.

After about five years what was originally envisioned as a

minor support function within the overall structure of the company had become the largest division in terms of budget and assets. Decisions at the top were now made with consideration given to IS—even ahead of the concerns of the manufacturing division! Soon, IS had its own stylish new building. By the time I left, the formerly blue-collar company had changed its name, and the manufacturing division had been phased out entirely.

N: *Basic Terms*

I tried to teach Hub some basic technology terms. Not surprisingly, he resisted—though he did make an effort at first.

"Okay, go ahead," he said finally, sitting back in his chair. "I need to sound credible when I explain to my easily impressed staff why the toys they want are *not* needed."

I started slowly, trying to explain the terms in ways he could relate to.

Me: "The **hard drive** is the part of the computer that stores your data. You'll probably come to know it as the device that freezes up whenever you touch anything."

Him: "You mean like that timid new secretary whenever I'm around?"

Me: "The **monitor** contains the screen, which flickers when you run into it with your briefcase."

Him: "Looks like a television, but not nearly as useful, right?"

Me: "A **CD** is a compact disc—"

Him: "Balderdash! A CD is a certificate of deposit, and I won't let anyone tell me differently. You've taken over enough of my American culture already."

After several minutes like this, I lost my patience and gave up. I left a copy of *Computers for Dunces* on his bookshelf and sought refuge among my own kind.

H: *My Own Interpretations*

- **Scanner:** Scanners used to come in handy during our late-night waste disposal runs. Now all they do is sit there on the table in silence.

- **Smart Board:** Few companies have one, so you're in

luck. If you do have to work with one, make sure you keep the members disconnected.

- **Chat:** A program that allows young people to form tremendously "serious" and "passionate" relationships with weirdos, foreigners, and other ne'er-do-wells that two months later they will have totally forgotten.

- **MP3:** A musical format that allows you to avoid paying for compact discs. Ironically, you then go and pay absurd ticket prices to see the same bands in concert.

- **Internet:** Something I managed to survive without, and so can you. Prior to my retirement, I was sternly corrected while visiting another firm that had its entire operation networked.

  "How do you control what your employees view on your Internet?" I asked.

  "We have an Int*r*anet not an Int*er*net," he corrected.

  Frankly, all I could see were a bunch of Inter*nuts*.

- **Dee VD:** Not sure. I kept hearing the techie foreigners asking everyone "Have you got dee VD?" Personally, I don't think it's any of their damn business.

- **Multitasking:** The ability to fail at multiple tasks simultaneously. The best example is driving. Fatalities caused by in-vehicle distractions now equal those of drunk driving. My father had a hat and gloves that he wore only when he went driving, because driving was a special activity all by itself. Nowadays, you put a kid in a car and tell him to focus solely on driving, and he can't do it. He's been scatter-brained his whole life, watching TV while playing a video game while talking on the phone—it's impossible for him to sit in that car and concentrate only on driving.

N: *Some Technology Acceptable After All*

"There's nothing wrong with our current productivity levels," Hub said as he frowned at the last computer salesman who dared to visit. "We don't need any new technology products. Who sent for you?"

"I did," I said as I stuck my head in the room. "I thought you might like to see the latest document shredders. They're running a special."

"Oh, well, yes . . . I might like to see one or two. Not that we really need one here, of course. But since you came all this way . . ."

H: *Beware Of Technology Searching For Applications*

With a very few exceptions, you don't have to own the latest gadgetry. Most of the technology out there looks clever during the demos, but in the real world is of little practical value. Picture phones are a good example. Working prototypes have drawn "oohs" and "ahs" from trade show audiences for years—yet, nobody wants the silly things. Here are other gee-whiz products that will never be more than curiosities.

- **Internet appliance:** I was almost fooled by the term "appliance." Then I learned this was *not* something useful like a dishwasher—which, at least, can double as a golf-ball washer. These are computers with no hard drive. All they do is connect to the Internet. (That's right—once the Internet dies out, these things won't even make good boat anchors.)

- **WebRV:** A motor home equipped with Internet terminals. (Just what somebody needs when he's trying to get away from it all.)

- **Scent generator:** A device that generates different scents based on input from a Web site. (Now people will have to install "odor eaters" on their computers to protect themselves.)

- **Virus detector:** Software that gets rid of known viruses on a system, which were forwarded via emails from friends. (Key word: "known." The most destructive viruses, of course, are *new* ones. I've got a better idea— simply keep the stupid computer turned *off*.)

- **Voice recognition:** Vice-controlled input software hat claims Yukon speak hat your normal place and achieve 98 percent accuracy. (My secretary used won instead of typing this sentry.)

- **Chess playing program:** A program that enables you to play chess with a computer. Has become the poster boy for artificial intelligence. (Let's see. The computer must consider *millions* of possible alternatives before it is able to make a sensible move. The human weighs only *a couple dozen* options before making an equally sensible move. Which one would you call intelligent?)

- **In-vehicle navigation system:** Satellite guidance system that displays your location relative to various restaurants and makes reservations for you. (For those of you who can't get a table without a reservation I suppose this might be of some use.)

- **Appointment scheduler:** Software that tracks your appointments and notifies you with messages and/or alarms. (Already had one. Her name was Nicole and she was anything but alarming.)

- **PDA:** A computer so tiny that users need a swizzle stick to type and a magnifying glass to read the screen. (Nicholas wanted one of these, but even he couldn't show me anything it did that was truly useful.)

- **Language translation:** Software that provides an approximate translation from a foreign language into English or vice versa. (Aren't they supposed to know English by now? They'll never learn it if we keep inventing programs like this one.)

- **Online stock trading:** A program that allows novices to buy and sell securities without the services of a broker. (We've all seen how well this can work, haven't we?)

- **Sports handicapper:** Tracks and analyzes dozens of variables, including road-away records, weather, injuries, performances against the spread, and so forth. Uploads latest odds from Las Vegas, then makes a prediction with 98 percent accuracy. (Now this would be something useful!)

H: *What Are The Odds?*

Speaking of odds, let's have a little fun. What are the chances that any of the following might happen?

- You catch your secretary shopping for clothes on the Internet when she's supposed to be typing that report for you. (1:2)

- A computer locks up at night, so you don't have to. (1:4)

- Within five years every word in the English language is preceded by the letter *e*—as in e-commerce, e-solutions, e-government, E. coli . . . (1:10)

- I start my own dot-com company. (1:1,000,000)

- The IS department sets up a secretary's new computer and never has to come back to reinstall anything. (1:100,000,000)

- Bill Gates wins a World Boxing Federation title by KO and kicks a 65-yard field goal into the wind to win the Super Bowl on the same day. (1:"Biggest number you can think of")

- Bill Gates publicly admits Microsoft is a monopoly. (1:"Biggest number you can think of" x 2)

N: *Environmental Stewardship*

"We keep high-tech products to a minimum at my company because of our ongoing concern for the environment," Hub told me one afternoon as he stood in his office and gestured out the window that overlooked the weedy retention pond.

"What about the stuff our plant is flushing down the drain?"

"It is well known that waste chemicals can be diluted in lakes and rivers. Eventually, the waterways will bounce back. But what do you do with computer monitors, printers, plotters, scanners, and the rest? Many landfills won't take them."

"There are recycling programs for schools and inner-city kids."

"Is there a tax write-off?"

"Yeah, I think so."

"Well, it's probably still not worth it. I've seen basements and storage areas at other companies packed with old equipment. Apparently not even the schools want it. I do give credit to that company I toured last week—they converted their old monitors into aquariums."

Actually, those fish were screen savers.

H: *Consumer Welfare*

Another reason my company avoids the latest technology is the "buggy" software that troubles the industry. Software developers knowingly send inferior, improperly tested products to market with little or no concern for consumer welfare. This in itself is acceptable if you price such products at a discount, but flawed high-tech products are generally sold at high markups.

N: *Compatibility Issues*

Even I have to give Hub some slack when it comes to compatibility. I was trying to troubleshoot a problem when he walked slowly past.

"More downtime?" he sputtered as he glanced over his shoulder.

"Yes, Mr. Ablebright," Amber, an administrative assistant, said seriously. "Version 6 of SuperTyper won't read files from SuperTyper 5 or SuperTyper 7."

"When you buy new golf balls you don't have to worry about whether they will work with the putter you already own," Hub declared. "Come to think of it, I wonder if *that* has been my problem lately . . ." he mused, then mimicked his putting stroke.

A while later he was circling again.

"You don't have the proper drivers loaded," I told Amber, who was now distraught over the printer problems she was having. "Plus, you're trying to do a female-to-female cable hookup when what you need is male-female."

"I've been trying to tell her that for weeks!" a winking Hub interrupted.

9

PUBLIC RELATIONS

H: *The Value Of "PR"*

Putting the proper "spin" on things probably goes against the grain of your generation, which prides itself on lampooning hypocrisy. This lack of appreciation for the value of public relations explains the poor image you have in the public eye. The "PR" for your age group has been poorly handled—consequently you are constantly being maligned.

Presenting yourself and your company as a forward-thinking, environmentally friendly, employee-sensitive, market-savvy, financially sound, community-concerned corporate citizen is a full-time task. No wonder so many companies dedicate entire departments to the process of public and media relations. You can make their job easier by being sure to consistently put your best foot forward.

Terms To Avoid	Better
layoffs	retrenchment
poor earnings	quiet revenues
sexual harassment	questionable conduct
product recalls	quality-assurance measures

corporate lobbying	participating in the process
hostile takeover	aggressive courtship
court order	judicial settlement
executive perks	market incentives
sweatshop	high-intensity production units
contaminated site	brownfield
strike	walkout

Put the "Terms To Avoid" in a sentence about your company and you'll see just how powerful words can be.

Look for new executive perks to be challenged after poor earnings, product recalls, and a costly sexual harassment suit led to the company's recent announcement of layoffs, which came on the heels of a hostile takeover bid that was stalled by a court order some critics say was spurred by corporate lobbying that offered in exchange the cleanup of a long-disputed contaminated site and the closing of Asian sweatshops, the latter of which will also hopefully calm recent strike threats.

On the other hand, that dire prognosis could have been described this way:

Look for new market incentives to be examined after quiet revenues, quality-assurance measures, and a costly questionable conduct suit led to the company's recent retrenchment, which came on the heels of an aggressive courtship that was interrupted by a judicial settlement some experts say was spurred by participating in a process that will lead to brownfield reclamation and the scaling back of high-intensity production units, the latter of which will also calm recent walkout scenarios.

N: *Media Treatment*

With all that PR and spin-doctoring, it's surprising how often executives are described negatively in the media. The following sound bites, culled from news sources such as the *Minneapolis Star Tribune, Milwaukee Journal Sentinel, USA Today*, and others, are typical descriptions of executives or their activities. I gave Hub a chance to respond to each. His comments are in parentheses.

- **". . . sharp, distant executive now reviled . . ."** (H: At least this implies there was a time when this exec was *not* reviled.)

- "... **blunt, two-fisted** ..." (H: Usually unfair, but could be a compliment in the right context.)

- "... **embattled** ..." (H: Fast becoming a cliché.)

- "... **scheme designed to enrich themselves and dupe shareholders** ..." (H: Hmm, tell me more. Just kidding!)

- "... **suave college dropout** ..." and "... **onetime seller of monkeys through the mail** ..." (H: Now what does *that* have to do with anything?)

- "... **conceited, pompous executive** ..." (H: How dare they!)

- "... **dominating, egocentric** ..." (H: A fellow who knows what he wants, that's all.)

- "... **executives must stop feathering their nests** ..." (H: Sure beats getting plucked.)

- "... **an eccentric executive accustomed to always getting his way** ..." (H: It's too bad our society now views getting what you want as eccentric.)

- "... **nine lives of ousted corporate fat cats** ..." (H: Nine? Don't be absurd. Three or four is plenty.)

- "... **corporate slugs got rich** ..." (H: Aren't slugs technically exempt from income tax?)

- "... **a boss who is off the wall—so crazed that he or she is a menace to your mental health** ..." (H: Did it ever occur to them how that boss became crazed in the first place?)

N: *Hollywood, Too*

The negative portrayals are not limited to the media. Hollywood also has it in for executives. Look at how executive characters are described in some reviews and promos.

Movie: *A Civil Action,* starring John Travolta and Sydney Pollack
Features a "... pompous executive with the corporation of W.R. Grace & Co."

Movie: *Behind Office Doors*
"A pompous executive has a hard time admitting that his hard-working, devoted secretary is really the one pulling the strings in his office and is behind his promotion to company president."

Movie: *King Kong,* starring Jeff Bridges and Charles Grodin
Features a ". . . pompous oil executive in search of fabled petroleum deposits . . ."

Movie: *What Women Want,* starring Mel Gibson and Helen Hunt
Features a ". . . pompous advertising executive dubbed the 'T&A King' for his successful reign over Swedish bikini-babe commercials."

Movie: *Mannequin*
The actor ". . . portrays his slimy executive as a pompous, stammering buffoon . . ."

Hub responded by exclaiming that it was little wonder that he hadn't been inside a movie theater since 1964. "Britney tried to fool me into seeing *Titanic* by telling me it had a surprise ending," he commented. "I told her I'd wait for the sequel."

H: *Questions At Live Press Conferences*

Speaking of the Titanic, here's where you'll sink for sure if you're not well prepared. As a young professional you will get to know the scene well. Standing in for your boss, you will be getting hounded at a press conference by the usual pack of bloodthirsty reporters and columnists (who each look at least fifteen years older than their photos in the newspaper). You'll look evasive in the public's eye if you keep saying, "No comment." A seasoned pro can do better. To buy time, first ask if everyone else heard the question clearly. Don't wait for an answer—just go ahead and take the opportunity to select an escape strategy and/or restate the question into a friendlier version if necessary.

> ### Example 1: Restate and reword.
> **Question:** "How does your company intend to reply to the recent allegations of misconduct?"
> **Answer:** "The question was, 'Do we intend to reply to the recent allegations of conduct?' Of course we will, once more information is made available. Next?"

Example 2: Focus on a marginal issue.

Question: "Your boss didn't answer this question in his television interview last night, so I'm going to ask it again today. Can we expect another round of layoffs soon?"

Answer: "That question wasn't even supposed to be a part of the discussion last night. The commentator broke his own ground rules. The question was totally out of context and totally unfair. Next?"

Example 3: Answer their questions with your own questions.

Question: "Your quarterly earnings reports have been disappointing for the last three quarters. How long do you expect this trend to continue?"

Answer: "Whose definition of 'disappointing' are we using? And when it comes to forecasting the future, who in this room is infallible?"

Example 4: Words have so many meanings—that's why we have dictionaries.

Question: "Your CEO recently remarked, 'In the beginning, God should have created *me*. Then the world wouldn't be in the mess it's in.' Did he really mean that?"

Answer: "Yes, he said that, but obviously there was something deeper he was trying to convey."

Example 5: Challenge longstanding assumptions.

Question: "Wouldn't the phrase, 'Absolute power corrupts absolutely' describe your CEO?"

Answer: "That phrase is self-contradictory and therefore has no validity. If corruption can overtake him, then he truly doesn't have absolute power, does he?"

Example 6: Pretend to be offended at the question, and then leave.

Question: "Have you explored using natural lighting at your new office complex?"

Answer: "I'm not going to dignify that question with an answer. I was going to be polite and pretend not to hear it, but no one should have to stand here and take this abuse. Good-bye."

N: *Press Leaks*

Preferring to play the role of reporter, I once asked Hub as we drove to the airport, "Why did you announce the layoffs by memo?"

"I was in a hurry—I didn't have time to orchestrate a press leak. Don't look so surprised. We'll be passing a billboard soon with some more names on it."

The sad thing is, I didn't know whether he was joking or not.

"Well, what do you expect?" he continued. "I suppose you'd send each one a fruit basket."

"A memo just seems kind of impersonal."

"Oh, I'm a big believer in the personal touch, but things get out of hand in a situation like this."

"What about an announcement at a group meeting then?"

"Ha!" he exclaimed, putting a hand on my shoulder. "I'll let you handle the next round, and then you'll know why I used a memo. The last place you want to be is in an enclosed room with a bunch of people who have just lost their jobs."

"Especially when they were told a month ago that everything was great."

"We have to do that to avoid sabotage."

There you have it. When you need to avoid a personal announcement in front of the targeted employees, a memo is fine, but a leak to the press is infinitely more effective. Once the news is out you can react with indignation that the story broke before you were able to announce it personally to your employees.

"Of course," continued Hub, "once the bad news becomes common knowledge, there's no point in re-announcing it at a company meeting. Simply issue an apologetic memo from the far-flung conference you're now attending and pin the blame on the preemptive news report. Refer all questions about outstanding sick leave, unemployment benefits, and related matters to your on-site staff."

H: *Articles, Interviews*

Who we are and what we do is by nature controversial. Big corporations are newsmakers. Handling the media in person is only half the battle, however. There may be fewer newspapers today than a few decades ago, but the few that remain can be pesky.

And, don't forget magazines. These days there seems to be a magazine dedicated to every conceivable topic. For every worthwhile monthly like *Golf Digest,* there are a dozen useless rags like *Escalator Etiquette* and *Musical Doorbell Composer.* They're all hungry for new stories and new angles. There are three possible strategies you could pursue to limit your exposure.

1) **Allow yourself to be interviewed in an effort to set the record straight.**

   (Okay, you can stop chuckling now.) As you already know, overlooked media types are constantly seeking ways to make a name for themselves, and your troubles send them off into fits of pleasure. The last thing they want to do is write a boring article describing how everything has been blown out of proportion and there's no smoking gun after all. To save themselves they will take one of your marginal comments if need be and run wild with it, creating an entirely new angle to keep the flames burning.

2) **Write your own press release or article and put your own spin on the events in question.**

   This sounds promising in theory, but unless you own the newspapers and magazines giving you the most grief, there's no way to guarantee they will publish it. Even if they do, by cleverly editing your wording and putting a sensational headline on it, they can actually make you incriminate yourself.

3) **Let things blow over.**

   Sad to say, this is probably the best you can do. Fortunately, people nowadays have wonderfully short attention spans—if they care at all anymore. You can also take comfort in the knowledge that there is strength in numbers. There are so many companies in hot water these days that your "scandal" will only make waves for a short time before it is swept away by the next storm of controversy.

N: *Sound Bites*

Older executives seem to prefer newspapers and magazines to television and radio. Hub himself confirmed it with desk-pounding certainty: "I have a lot of important things to say on most occasions, and I don't like being cut off or edited, which is always the treatment people like me get from the big-haired TV and radio types." Then, he sat back and added in a quieter tone, "For inexperienced professionals like you who have little to say, however, sound bites might be best."

With that advice in mind, we will probably want to stick to television and radio, where shallowness is actually encouraged. Here is an exchange between Hub and a consultant who gave a presentation on communication skills to the Ablebright office staff at an in-house seminar.

"A sound bite," the consultant began, "is an art form that includes the following traits: It's brief, catchy, enhances your image or position on an issue, appears spontaneous, and sounds plausible when first heard."

"Give me an example," Hub asked the consultant warily.

"Okay, here's one. 'If government reduced corporate tax rates, my business could pass the savings on to consumers.'"

Hub rubbed his chin thoughtfully. "Hey, I kind of like that one. Do you have any more?"

10

BUSINESS TRAVEL

H: *Simplicity*

Drifting about with no deadline or destination, hanging around the homes of friends and relatives, or dumping your backpack on a cot in a hostel are all fine and dandy if you're one of those students forever between classes. Anybody can see it won't do for a smart young professional who wants to be successful. Instead, you need to prepare yourself for the hassles of travel that come with having to be somewhere on time.

Once I rose to the level of CEO, I generally avoided the ordeal by insisting that other people come to me. You, however, are not yet so lucky. Your early years will likely include plenty of airlines, hotel rooms, and restaurants. My key in reducing inconveniences was to seek simplicity. I'll loan you an acronym I invented when I was younger to remind me of this objective: KIASAYPCS (Keep It As Simple As You Possibly Can, Stupid). In a pinch, the acronym can be shortened to KIASAPS (Keep It As Simple As Possible, Stupid).

H: *Tips On Tipping*

Seldom is the simplicity principle more important than when it comes to tipping. Just between you, me, and the fence post, who-ever started this foolishness should be "tipped" off the nearest cliff. I don't know about you, but I had plenty to worry about already—I didn't want to be trying to remember who got how much and when.

Take a gander at all these people wanting a handout.

Doorkeeper: $1 for hailing a cab that nearly ran me over.

Bellhop: $1 per carelessly tossed bag.

Valet: $1 to retrieve a car that he wore out the brakes on.

Waiter: 15 to 20 percent for helping me run up an exorbitant bill.

Bartender: 10 percent for watering down my drinks.

Courtesy van driver: $1 for not being courteous.

Cab drivers: 15 percent for getting lost.

Limousine chauffeur: 20 percent of the exorbitant tab.

Tour guide: $3 a day for boring me to tears.

N: *Don't Leave Anyone Out*

Hey, don't forget these often neglected service-industry employees.

Beekeeper: $1 per sting.

Dishwasher: 25¢ for each spot-free glass.

Plumber: $5 (minus $1 per inch of butt crack showing).

Gravedigger: $1 per foot.

Car radio DJ: $1 per hour (stick tip into slot above radio).

Magazine attendant in laundromat: $1 for each current year issue.

H: *Tipping Continued*

If it were up to me, I'd have skipped the whole thing. However, for the sake of my company image I played along—but under my rules. I simply tipped everybody $5 across the board. I realize this policy meant that some people would be shortchanged. Then again, it also meant some got extra, so everything evened out in the end. The waitress who got less from me probably got more than usual from the baggage handler who came in for lunch, because he had extra change in his pocket from the time I *over*-tipped him.

N: *Helping Things "Even Out"*

I think Hub's strategy was called "trickle sideways economics." Nevertheless, I found that those poor waitresses had a much better chance of receiving their due if I tossed a few extra bills on the table after Hub turned to leave. I had to be careful, though, because one time I spotted Hub pocketing my extra tip when he went back to the table to pick up a pen he had supposedly left behind.

H: *Meet Your Party*

Believe me, if I had ever done that kind of thing, I would have been subtle enough to escape notice—and here's the proof. There have been times when temporary company belt-tightening measures forced me to fly commercial airlines or take the train to a meeting with new clients. Since we had never met face-to-face, a welcoming committee was usually on hand holding up a sign to identify themselves. I would pretend not to notice. Since they didn't know me, I could take up a position close to them, as though waiting for somebody else, and in each case they had no idea I was their man.

As the time passed I was often able to overhear certain ill-advised comments that were later used to my advantage.

- Sign-holder looking at his watch and mumbling to himself: "Where is that dumb son-of-a-bitch?"

- Associate: "Hold the sign up higher. Maybe the old fart can't see very well."
  Sign-holder, grinning: "Or he's too plastered to read it."

- Associate calls office on cell phone: "We're in luck—the gasbag didn't make it."

The looks on their faces when I introduced myself were priceless.

N: *Priceless*

Here are a few additional "priceless" items when you're on the road.

New duffel bag that must be kept on your lap because it won't fit in the overhead storage compartment: $80

Round-trip tickets to Japan and seat assignment between two out-of-shape Sumo wrestlers: $1,200
Getting bumped to the next flight: Priceless.

Carton of motion sickness tablets for in-flight turbulence: $7
Bottle of aspirin for headache caused by nearby screaming baby: $6
Emergency landing on South Pacific island known for soothing volcanic springs: Priceless.

Hearty lunch to fill the void left by the hotel's complimentary continental breakfast: $15
Thin-walled hotel room where you can hear physical activities in neighboring rooms: $95
False fire alarm at midnight that sends half-naked women running into hallways: Priceless.

Curried Cajun Hot Chili Pepper Sandwich Supreme that your friends dared you to order: $12
Bottle of beer to put out the fire: $3
Hub finally cornered into buying a round at the bar: Priceless.

Anti-terrorism training for personal security guards: $70,000
Satellite hookup and company video conferencing center: $50,000
VIPs who remain home to protect their assets: Worthless.

H: *The Waiting Game*

No matter what kind of travel arrangements you make, you can bet your last cup of Folgers that you're going to be delayed somewhere, somehow. The key is to make some use of this downtime so it's not entirely wasted. I offer below one of my favorite strategies for passing the time in an amusing manner.

Situation: Sitting in an airport waiting for an overdue connection.

I always carried along a year-old *USA Today* and set it in a place where other waiting travelers would notice it. Sure enough, several people would pick it up and start reading. It was a delight to watch how long they continued to read before noticing something wasn't right. Often it took several minutes. After all, the news is mostly recycled anyway. There's always trouble in the Middle East, gasoline prices are frequently threatening to rise, and a flood, earthquake, or ferry boat sinking is usually occurring someplace.

More often than not, they'd read the entire paper, although with each page turn a faint expression of puzzlement grew across their brows. Some readers shifted in their seats and became downright agitated when they saw a favorite stock or ball team they thought was on the rebound bottoming out again. Others showed a bewildered but pleased look as they saw a $10 dog they should have sold at $30 suddenly at $34. Either way, the entertainment value sure can't be topped.

N: *Starbucks*

Hub and I were walking along an airport concourse, waiting for a client to arrive, when Hub stopped abruptly and gestured toward one of the Starbucks shops.

"I went in one of those places once," he said. "Tried to get a cup of black coffee with sugar. Best they could do was a plastic cup full of some slop called Komodo Dragon Blend. I suppose your bunch spends quite a bit of time inside those joints."

As was often his habit, Hub started forward again and didn't wait for me to catch up or respond.

"I'll grant you, they're pretty hard to avoid, since they're damn near everywhere. Heck, you see that fat guy over there? Starbucks will soon be opening another store—for the people on the other side of him."

I queued up and played my standard courtesy laugh for him.

"You don't patronize those places—do you?" he asked me again.

"Patronize?"

"Frequent."

"Frequent?"

"Visit . . . go to!" he barked.

"Oh, now I read you. No, not usually. But the poor guy had to do something after they canceled *Battlestar Gallactica*."

"I don't follow. What do you mean by that Gallactistar thing?"

"Oh, sorry. That was just a TV show with a character named Starbuck."

"Oh, I see."

"Good, because I don't have a pencil with me."

"What for?"

"To connect the dots for you."

"I'll fix you later," he muttered.

H: *Beggars Can't Be Choosy*

Nicholas liked to think he could get me riled, but nothing got under my skin more than a beggar or con artist working the crowd at the airport. Some pretended to be blind or dumb, and still others dragged pathetic urchins along with them who looked like characters out of a bad Dickens novel.

I made it my habit to listen sympathetically to their pitch, and then I smiled as I reached into my pocket, pulled out a card with a penny taped to it, and handed it to them. The card read, "May this good-luck penny bring you fortune and fame." I never saw any of the recipients successfully hide their disappointment.

N: *He Had A Lot Of Pennies*

I heard that he pulled the same routine on employees asking for raises.

H: *Simple Solution*

Fed up with tasteless airline food? Bring along your own chef. Tired of waiting for connecting flights? Always fly nonstop and do it around *your* schedule. Exhausted from sitting on the tarmac for three hours? Fly out of small regional airports where waiting is minimal. All you need is your own jet.

I remember precisely when I made the decision I would never fly commercial again. I had taken my seat next to a casually dressed, clean-cut man about 50 years old who had the window seat. I settled in and waited for the rest of the passengers to file in and the stewardesses to stow everything away and make their announcements. None of the stewardesses were particularly attractive, so I turned my attention to the passenger sitting next to me.

This fellow proved to be a difficult nut to crack. His responses to my initial forays were short, staccato bursts, accompanied by movements that were sudden and almost jerky, like a nervous animal might make. As I watched him further, his hand wringing, his constant glances out the window and then up toward the cockpit, and so forth, it finally occurred to me that this was probably the poor fellow's first flight. In an effort to reassure him, I leaned over and said I'd flown dozens of times without incident and flying was actually safer than driving your own car.

He glanced back at me with a slightly condescending scowl and muttered, "I know. I'm a commercial pilot."

My jaw dropped. I quickly turned back toward the aisle. Now *I* was the one doing the hand wringing. If this flight veteran was apprehensive about doing something he probably did every other day, what did he know that I didn't? What was out there on the wing that he kept studying? What did he know about the cockpit?

Yessir, that did it for me. If one of their own couldn't even relax . . . it was time to make other arrangements.

H: *How To Pack*

I always got a warm, fuzzy feeling when I saw the crew loading my golf clubs onto my private jet. In the old days I used to worry about packing extra underwear and socks in my carry-on just in case my luggage was lost by overpaid baggage handlers "doing what we do best."

Your generation has done its share of traveling, so I hardly need to warn you about the tribulations you'll face. You already know that the overnight toiletry bag the airline gives you when you're stranded doesn't include condoms.

The airlines, however, should not shoulder all of the blame for delays and poor service. Part of the problem is the burden placed upon them by demanding passengers who think they are entitled to bring along practically everything they own. Can't you go more than one block from your apartment without bringing along *all* of your compact discs? Trust me, they've got Limp Bizkit wherever you're going.

H: *Gourmet Dining*

Speaking of biscuits, once you're back on the ground, you'll eventually have to eat. Traveling executives either dine at the finest gourmet restaurants in town or they order room service. Most young professionals, used to food fights in college cafeterias, are generally unprepared for an experience where servers outnumber patrons. And yes, it is still possible for an establishment without a drive-thru to be a restaurant. The last place I dined was a fairly typical experience, so I will share it with you.

In an ordinary restaurant you are herded to a booth and given a menu listing dozens of food choices—then immediately asked whether you would like anything to *drink*. With nothing to guide your selection, you try to order a decent wine, which they seldom have, but how are you to know? So what *do* they have? The waitress rattles off the choices so fast you can only choose the one name you heard clearly and can remember. Contrast this with a five-star restaurant, where the maitre d' takes you slowly through the dining room so you can be properly seen, seats you at a table, and has the decency to ask whether you would like to look at a wine list.

After the wine order has been placed with the wine steward, your waiter (or sometimes a chef if your table is important enough) appears to describe the "specials." This person takes this duty as seriously as an announcement of the end of the world, and so should you. Listen attentively and nod and smile as though you've never heard anything described so delectably before. In reality, of course, the waiter frequently speaks with an accent and babbles on at length about incomprehensible creations containing "lovely béarnaise bonbons spread over a delightful au jus sauce steeped in sultry stewed lemon peelings and served over domesticated Pakistani rice cakes." Even if you had any inclination to try such a dish, by the time he's finished all you want is something simple that you can pronounce, like a hot dog. Nevertheless, you should exclaim that the special sounds exquisite, but you'd like to see a menu (because everybody knows these specials are simply mishmashes of oddball ingredients the chef is trying to get rid of).

You will probably be dismayed to find the menu is nearly as incomprehensible as the list of specials. If handled improperly, the situation can become rather embarrassing.

"Go ahead, Nicholas, you can order first," I announced.

"I'll have the, um . . ."

"For mercy's sake, don't point at the item like a child."

I winked at Harry, VP of marketing, as Nicholas shifted uncomfortably in his chair. "I'll try the . . . the Oofs in Murett."

"Ah, the Oeufs en Meurette. A fine selection," said the waiter, who hid his amusement reasonably well.

Obviously, if you have a choice you will let others order before you, so that you can listen to how they pronounce various items (or how the waiter re-pronounces them) and then order something similar.

N: *Gourmet Dining, Part Two*

That waiter may have known how to hide his amusement, but I'll bet his expression spoke volumes when he totaled Hub's tip.

I'll never forget the time Derek, Janelle, and I were along with Hub and a client at a classic five-star place in Boston. We had just been seated when the client and Hub embarked on some serious negotiating. They both got up and went back to the office, leaving the three of us sitting there.

"Let's have a little fun," Derek said, sitting back and cracking his knuckles. "Let's break every stupid etiquette rule in the book."

Janelle's nose twitched and she laughed nervously, as she always did when she got excited. "What'll we do?"

"We can start by ordering a dessert wine," I suggested, "if our waiter ever bothers to come to our table again." I tried flagging one down.

Derek finally grabbed one who looked like Ichabod Crane. *"Do you know who I am?"* Derek said indignantly, borrowing one of Hub's lines.

Our waiter was a bit patronizing as he described the specials.

Derek interrupted him. "Don't you have, like, mac and cheese or something?"

Startled for only an instant, the waiter continued on.

We finally ordered, and when the soup came we slurped. We ordered one Caesar salad and passed it around. We put our elbows on the table and gnawed on the bread like peasants. We devoured our sorbet palate cleansers, licking the lily dishes clean with our tongues. Derek blew his nose into his napkin right there at the table in front of God and everyone. The city had seldom seen such bold and naked atrocities.

The scandalized patrons turned and raised their eyebrows disapprovingly. Janelle belched proudly in response.

The waiter came around and asked with mock concern how everything was.

"A lot better than we expected," I said.

"Could I have more sorbet?" Janelle asked, holding up her lily dish. "I don't think my pallet is cleansed yet. What do you think, Nicholas?" she asked and turned to me with her mouth gaping wide.

I peered inside with the concern of a dentist and shook my head disapprovingly. "That's one filthy pallet, no doubt about it."

I'll tell you, we sure received fast service after that. They had our entrees on our table in no time, and the bill immediately thereafter.

N: *Lodging*

Let's leave dining behind and talk about sleeping. Only the wealthiest executives have a house in every city. The rest of us have to settle for a regular room at the conference rate. Hub always stayed in a hotel suite near the convention center, but I recommend places off the beaten path. Small hotels and inns have more character and make for a way more interesting stay.

"I don't know why you want to stay someplace else," Hub always warned me. "At least try to avoid places where kids stay free, the television in your room is bolted to the wall, or the lobby is used to host starving artists sales."

I am usually drawn to establishments advertising "historic ambiance" or "antique furnishings." These are code words for "hasn't been updated since the 1950s." Perfect! For little more than the price of a carton of cigarettes I get . . .

- Ashtrays.

- Mattresses so sunken in the middle that nothing escapes, not even light.

- Feather pillows so flat and hard they must be stuffed with Pterodactyl feathers.

- See-through blankets so thin they were rejected by the troops at Valley Forge.

- A large, white bathtub that may have been used to ferry Washington's troops across the Potomac. (Includes rudder-like faucet and curtain that might have doubled as a sail.)

- A toilet with so many chains to pull that I feel like a monk ringing the bells at Westminster Abbey.

- A Gideon Bible so old and tattered it has "Property of Gideon" scrawled inside the front cover.

- Dusty postcards for sale in the gift shop that show the hotel in its heyday, when there were pink 1957 Chevy's parked out front.

H: *International Travel*

I didn't want Nicholas to embarrass me on our first trip overseas together, so I collared him in the limo on the way to the airport.

"The standard pabulum goes something like this," I told him: 'We Americans must be extra courteous and sensitive to others while we are abroad. When in Rome, do as the Romans do.' This makes absolutely no sense. Do you think residents of Germany or England or Sweden want to host visitors awkwardly trying to act like the Germans, English, or Swedes they see every day? Of course not. They want to see an American act like an American. They are fascinated by our culture and are universally disappointed when we don't portray the image they are expecting."

N: *Postscript*

Immediately after this little speech, I asked Hub whether we were going to stop in at Yodaco's headquarters during our trip.

"What do you care about them? They're just a little two-bit operation with a couple of employees. Nothing worth seeing, believe me."

Hmmm. According to Serena, this "two-bit operation," as Hub called it, managed to burn through $22 million last year.

Hub suddenly leaned forward and instructed the limo driver to take a shortcut.

"It says 'Do Not Enter,'" the driver said as he slowed the vehicle.

"Don't worry about that—just go!" Hub directed.

If you ever become a traveling executive, you, too, will see that things like road signs are a nuisance justifiably dismissed by VIPs with more important things to worry about.

"I am thinking about a whistle stop in Bermuda, though," Hub said, lowering his voice so the driver wouldn't hear. "We could save millions in federal taxes by setting up our headquarters there. And, it wouldn't cost us much more than a post office box."

"I didn't know you could do that."

"Oh, yes. In fact, I put another call in to our lobbyist this morning to keep after our senators. We need to even the playing field with our overseas competitors."

Let's see, I guess that means that if in the next few years overseas companies manage to tilt the playing field to the point that they are liable for *zero* taxes, "our senators" will have to act again to keep things fair.

"What if they don't even the playing field?" I asked. "We'd have to move our entire operation to a country that was more fair, right?"

"That's what we'll threaten them with if we have to."

"But we'd never find room on Bermuda for all of our state-of-the-art plants, warehouses, runways, rails, roads, trained workforce and other infrastructure."

"Don't worry about all that. Just the threat of us leaving will be enough," Hub said confidently.

11

SALES & ADVERTISING

H: *The Salesman*

The steady, bulldogged salesman is a hero of a bygone era. He could sell anything from bristle replacements for brushes to polish for shower curtain rings. Yes, he was a bit quirky (his ties rarely matched his polyester suits), but that was part of his charm. The best among them won trips to Las Vegas for surpassing their quotas, while the rest toiled in unsung obscurity. I am proud to say I got my start as a humble salesman.

Viewed by younger generations, the salesman of the past is derided as a phony schmoozer of average intelligence at best. Whether he needed it or not, he has been given a Madison Avenue makeover to bring him up to the standards of the "hip" generation. Now he's known as a "marketing representative" or a "sales associate."

N: *Driving The Economy*

No doubt, the foundation of our economy relies on the purchase of necessities like appliances, automobiles, groceries, and health-care products. But the difference between bust and boom is the purchasing of luxuries like the SaladShooterUpper, Taco Belly Supremes, boxed Fats Whitman CD collections, and Pet Chia Rocks.

Even if you don't sell any products or services directly, there's a good chance you could end up creating marketing strategies, designing promotional materials, or supporting other functions that are part of a corporate brand. Do not blow off such assignments. Millions of families across this great land owe their good life in the suburbs to profits generated from Huggies, Mellow Yellow, Count Chocula, Grecian Formula, the Wonderbra, Baggies, and similar products.

H: *Everybody's An Expert*

I wish I had a nickel for every Dale Carnegie copycat out there holding seminars and writing books on how to sell anything to anyone. If they're so good why are they still hawking their wares? They ought to be retired on a duty-free Caribbean island by now.

Some of the symbols and analogies they attempt to use as teaching tools border on the ridiculous. Even Jesus isn't sacred. At least one "guru" tries to show how we can learn from the sales techniques used to "market" the gospel. Is there a historical figure, force of nature, or wild animal they haven't borrowed?

To prove a point, I will now proceed to show that it is possible to take virtually anything and draw lessons from it. I randomly selected a subject from the set of encyclopedias I keep in my study at home. I selected volume "H" and turned to page 267, where I found . . . "hummingbird." Let's see what treasures of knowledge rookie sales reps can glean from this tiny bird.

- *Thanks to remarkable memories, hummingbirds return to the same feeding sources year after year.*
  Lesson: Always remember that your best customers are repeat customers.

- *Male hummingbirds do not help raise their offspring.*
  Lesson: Plenty of long hours and travel means you'll be home late most nights.

- *Hummingbirds hover because they can flap their wings horizontally.*
  Lesson: Don't leave until the customer signs on the

dotted line. Too many rookies lose sales because they fly off in search of the next client before they've closed the previous deal.

- *According to an Indian legend, hummingbirds bring good luck and fair weather.*
  Lesson: Strive to cultivate an image that clients associate with good fortune. They will more readily welcome your arrival and heed your pitch.

- *The wings of some hummingbirds create a high-pitched buzz that is audible nearly 100 yards away.*
  Lesson: Create a buzz for your products that will attract attention even before you arrive in town.

- *Hummingbirds possess only fifty taste buds. (Humans have about 10,000.)*
  Lesson: Bad taste is a key prerequisite to being a successful sales rep.

- *Hummingbirds do not fly in flocks. They migrate alone.*
  Lesson: Sometimes it's just you against the world.

- *The tip of a hummingbird's tongue is long and brushy, allowing it to suck nectar from far inside a flower.*
  Lesson: Things can get interesting when you're out on the road in a strange city at night.

- *Hummingbirds enter a state of torpor on some nights to conserve energy.*
  Lesson: Actually, this is more applicable to my former third-shift plant workers than sales reps.

- *To survive, hummingbirds must drink almost twice their weight in nectar every day.*
  Lesson: The three-martini lunch is a fact of life when you're entertaining certain clients.

- *Some hummingbird species may fly more than 2,000 miles from wintering grounds in Mexico to reach nesting sites as far away as Alaska.*

Lesson: As the saying goes, "To convert the heathen, you have to go to the jungle." Good salesmen collect plenty of frequent-flier miles.

- *To match a hummingbird's huge daily appetite, a 180-pound person would need to eat about 204,000 calories.*
  Lesson: If you're not hungry, you're not going to be successful.

- *Hummingbirds can fly upside down if necessary because they beat their wings differently than other birds.*
  Lesson: It pays to be flexible. There are times you may have to stand on your head to get that sale.

- *During courtship, male ruby-throated hummingbirds may beat their wings up to 200 times per second.*
  Lesson: If the pursuit of the deal doesn't excite you, you're in the wrong field.

- *Hummingbirds can drive hawks away by outmaneuvering them.*
  Lesson: Your company may be small, but that doesn't mean you can't beat the big boys.

Well, that ought to be enough to prove my point. There is no shortage of cockamamie advice out there and an endless variety of approaches. You can pattern yourself after Genghis Khan, P.T. Barnum, the eagle, or the hummingbird if you like. What matters in the end is how much money you make and how quickly you make it.

N: *Re: The Hummingbird Sales Rep*
I've got to hand it to Hub on that one. I honestly didn't think he was that creative. I must be having an effect on him.

H: *Advertising Options*
The only good thing about the Internet is that it's a new way to advertise. Currently, we have available in our arsenal television, radio, movies, videos, telemarketing, direct mail, newspapers,

magazines, phone books, billboards, racing cars, blimps, airplane banners, rotating stadium signs, sandwich boards, handbills, balloons, business cards, buttons, stickers, matchbooks, T-shirts and caps, novelty items, and sponsorships. The Internet finally gives us a way to replace the town crier, a void that had gone unfilled for too long.

Older generations grew up appreciating advertising as a luxury. We were so happy to own a radio or television that we cherished the sponsorship announcements that made it all possible. We felt so privileged to be able to read that we studied newspaper ads simply for the pure enjoyment of reading. A call from a salesman at the door, especially in the rural countryside, was cause for excitement. Here was a chance to see a stranger from the city and be courted by a fancy new vacuum cleaner.

Furthermore, we admired corporations back then, companies like RCA, General Electric, Westinghouse, Sears & Roebuck, General Mills, and Mutual of Omaha. They were like part of our families. Wives trusted the advice the good folks at Montgomery Ward gave about the girdles they needed to control their figures. Children got the iron their blood needed because they heeded the counsel Nabisco offered about Cream of Wheat. Husbands and fathers counted on the insights Groucho Marx shared with them about the DeSoto's "fluid torque drive." And our elderly relatives stayed active because they listened to Lawrence Welk and took their Geritol.

Younger generations seem offended by commercial intrusions. Ever cynical, they have grown up taking the world for granted. If only once they had the opportunity to live through a real economic depression, how their outlook would change. Forever after, the ring of the cheerful telemarketer at dinnertime would be welcomed. The rows of billboards on the highway would become pleasant reminders of the return to prosperity. And, the boisterous commercials interrupting favorite shows would confirm again the nation's health.

Instead, your generation subjects companies to the worst kind of humiliation: Scrutiny.

"I found a better value on printing supplies," Nicholas informed me one day. "I got some good info through one of the newsgroups I'm on."

"What's wrong with the vendor I'm using? I've ordered from him for the last ten years. Fred and I play golf."

"They haven't been making their delivery times. A couple of times we've been caught short on supplies. Plus, I think they're stiffing us on the price for paper."

This skepticism can readily be traced back to the period when your parents tried to sell you the bill of goods that nothing would change after the divorce. The aftermath has left you unwilling to rely on the simple and direct word of anyone, including advertisers. Ever wary, your friends analyze every purchase through the exacting eyes of *Consumer Reports*. Nonetheless, even your generation has its weaknesses and can be sold with the right pitch.

N: *The Right Pitch?*

We don't like to be "sold." By the way, what *is* this pitch anyway?

H: *The Psychology Of The Ad Man*

Getting people to buy things they need is simple. Getting them to spring for items they *don't* need requires insight into human psychology. Effective advertisers master all of the powers of persuasion, because mere falsehoods are not always enough. Take the lady I saw advertising in the "Women Seeking Men" Personals: "Beautiful long legs. 5' 11" 185 lbs." It's probably more like 195. At those dimensions I'd hate to see the shape of what's on top of those long legs. Miss Humpty needs another angle if she's hoping for a dashing knight to come along and take her down from that wall. Her champion probably won't be the guy I saw advertising on the next page: "For Sale: One wife who let herself go. Free—if you haul her away." Now there's honesty if you want it.

Keep these important principles in mind when you participate in a marketing campaign.

1) **Principle:** People who are convinced they'll lose something if they don't quickly make a commitment are more likely to buy.

   Target: *Middle-aged.* They already think they have it all, so when they find out they're missing something, they'll be quick to buy it.

Won't Work: *Young.* They would rather lose everything than make a commitment

2) Principle: Shoppers are more motivated by their emotions than their rational intellect.

Target: *Young.* Lacking sufficient experience to judge wisely, they rely on feelings, which makes them especially ripe for the picking.

3) Principle: The pull of human curiosity is difficult for most people to resist.

Target: *All ages.* I don't know why this is, and I really don't care. (I guess I'm one of those special few who can resist this tremendous pull.)

4) Principle: Americans want bargains but not cheapness. They feel they deserve the best, but they don't want to have to pay full price for it.

Target: *Old.* They've sacrificed enough already and deserve their discounts.

Won't Work: *Middle-aged.* They prefer to pay premium prices just to show others that they can afford to.

5) Principle: An expensive price will automatically cause people to hold even junk in a higher regard.

Target: *Young.* For proof, just ask them what they paid for the clothing they're wearing.

6) Principle: Brands that boldly invite comparisons fare better than those that don't.

Target: *Middle-aged.* Since they are the surest of themselves, they admire products that convey a similar confidence.

The next time you're at the mall, see if you can spot these principles in action. My guess is you probably won't. Advertisers today mistakenly rely on glitz, the bizarre, and special effects to sell products. As a result, commercials are more likely to feature

some guy chasing down a cheetah and pulling a soda can out of
its throat. Apparently advertisers view your generation's fear of
commitment as a sign of shallowness, which they try to appeal to
through shallow marketing campaigns. Not surprisingly, the results are usually mixed at best.

In the Golden Age of Advertising, ad men appealed to one of
humanity's strongest instincts: The desire to avoid embarrassment. Just try to resist these two marketing masterpieces from
days gone by.

- **Old newspaper ad for Listerine Antiseptic pictur-
  ing a girl on the beach and a handsome boy ignor-
  ing her as he walks past:**

  There he was . . . that wonderful boy she met last night
  at the hotel dance! Suzanne uncorked her most glamor-
  ous smile, batted her most luscious lashes. No recognition. She waved her shapeliest arm, "yoo-hoo-ed" her
  most musical "yoo-hoo." No response. All of a sudden it
  dawned on her that he was deliberately giving her the
  air . . . *and was it frigid!*

That girl must have had *some* bad breath for a strapping
young man to resist a musical yoo-hoo *and* a shapely arm. How
many impressionable young people then and now would immediately run out and purchase Listerine to protect them from similar
humiliating moments? A helluva lot more than if the ad had featured Listerine being pulled out of a cheetah.

- **Old magazine ad for Lifebuoy Deodorant Soap de-
  picting a businessman being shunned by two of
  his associates, who are whispering in the doorway
  behind him:**

  No one is safe. Nothing can ruin chances of social and
  business success more quickly than "B.O." Even the
  faintest hint of it is enough to turn others against you.

I'll tell you right now, I'd get the hint. They wouldn't have to
warn *me* twice. Unfortunately, people today have become so sensitive that marketers have to be very careful about everything

they put out there. For example, soda companies trying to spur sales by running "Instant Winner!" contests got into trouble with the politically correct crowd when some of their bottle caps read, "Sorry, you're a loser." They quickly changed the wording to "Sorry, you're not a winner." That still caused an epidemic of clinical depression, so they depersonalized the wording even further until it read, "Sorry, *this bottle* is not a winner. Please be assured that this is probably no reflection on you personally."

N: *Let Me Try*

Hub inspired me to take a stab at my first marketing piece.

SnackyCakes Add First Ever Readable Ingredient

"We are extremely proud of this moment," beamed Maryann Scott, vice president for Healthy Treat Foods, as she held a souvenir SnackyCakes wrapper. "Today marks the first time in the storied history of SnackyCakes that mothers shopping for their families, dads shopping for lunch, and children looking for an after-school treat will be able to understand one of the ingredients on the SnackyCakes package."

The new ingredient, "wood," will not replace any of the existing essential ingredients. "We were simply looking for a little more firmness," said Scott. "Consumers will not notice any other changes. The same great SnackyCakes taste will remain as you've come to expect."

Ten-year-old Jeremy Robbins, attending the ceremony held at the Healthy Treat Thrift Store, apparently verified Scott's claims by gulping down his fourth SnackyCake in less than a minute.

"Knowing they've added a natural ingredient to my son's favorite snack gives me one less thing to worry about," added Jeremy's mother, Ruth.

H: *A Legend*

Nicholas has a long way to go before he reaches the level of Mel "The Closer" Hamsterdam. I've known several legendary salesmen in my career, but none as brilliant as Mel. He could sell gasoline and a match to Smokey the Bear. He started every day by downing three cups of coffee and proclaiming, "The fish sees the bait, not the hook." Then he'd grab his Abe Lincoln hat and cane and stride out the door.

Every great salesman has a gimmick, and that clever "Honest Abe" bit was Mel's. He kept a horse and carriage out back, and he'd ride it to all of his major customers. He'd stop at the client company's entrance, then wait for his attendant to open the carriage door, roll out a red carpet, and begin playing "Glory, Glory Hallelujah" on a trumpet. With a flourish he'd stride into the company president's office and announce, "Honest Abe is here to make you a deal!" Worked every time.

Nicholas met him once and was speechless.

12

THE PLANT

H: *A Different World*

The noisy manufacturing plants, gritty shipping and receiving docks, and gray warehouses of many companies are a different world from the quiet and cultured atriums and offices of the corporate campus. The contrast is almost as stark as the one that existed between the courts of Europe and the primitive Americas at the time of Cortez. You will find this comparison to be a useful one as you become acquainted with the customs of your rank-and-file workers.

For example, while you should never venture to the previously mentioned outposts alone, you will be perfectly safe in a small group, despite encountering substantially larger numbers. Like the natives of Cortez's day, the factory floor workers possess an instinctive awe and apprehensiveness when in the presence of men wearing suits. The early conquistadors wore crosses rather than ties, but like them you will be able to intimidate with a firm display of intelligence and authority.

N: *Red Ties The Most Powerful*

I shudder to think what might happen if I ever found myself lost in the wilds of the plant without my trusty red tie to ward off the inhabitants.

H: *What A Sight*

Tie or not, before you venture too frequently into the blue-collar world, it is best to learn the traits and behaviors of the plant's inhabitants. Almost instantly you will notice they are not like you in their appearance. I frequently spotted them milling about the assembly line, clad in Metallica T-shirts, Harley-Davidson caps, and oily black boots. They smelled of tobacco and other substances. Those were the chicks. The men were distinguished by the chain wallets in their back pockets and the oversized Colt 45 belt buckles straining to hold in their beer guts. Both genders sported Willie Nelson-style bandanas, tattoos, missing teeth, and scars in unusual places.

In the parking lot you will search in vain for shiny SUVs and BMWs. Instead there are rows of muddy Ford pickups, dented Dodge trucks, and jacked-up Chevy 4x4s. Among these testosterone-fueled vehicles crouch flame-painted muscle cars of various domestic makes, their oversized engines growling. The tangle of gearless, rusted bicycles bunched together in a heap are the property of the workers who have had their driver's licenses suspended.

At shift change, rock 'n' roll anthems from groups with names like Sticks, or mournful ballads from countrified belles like Shania Twang, bellow from tape players as vehicles roar off to the nearest tavern or quick-mart in search of cigarettes and lottery tickets. The less ambitious head straight home to their trailers for a night of WWF pageantry or sitcom repeats. The women who are not already divorced will nag and fight with their "old man," and the men who somehow still have a girlfriend will blacken one of her eyes to show "the bitch" they still care.

H: *What Makes Them Tick*

Of greater importance to you, however, are the differences between us and them on the *inside*.

For starters, there are the obvious differences in taste. For recreation you and I watch Formula One racing through our binoculars or play a little golf at Hilton Head. Plant workers prefer to camp outside Talladega and howl at NASCAR crashes or bowl a few balls down the alley between beer frames. For vacations you will fly off to explore Europe, while I sip tea in Bermuda. They'll follow a convoy to Branson or attend a gun show in Montana. You will someday be christening your children Warren or Chelsea. They'll call their kids Dale and Nadine. (Though it rarely occurs, crossbreeding between these two classes can have tragic consequences for the offspring. One couple I knew eventually broke up—as anyone could have predicted—and left a bewildered child in search of his identity. Last I heard, Jethro had left the Harvard Business School after only one semester to open a monster-truck driving school on Martha's Vineyard.)

The rank-and-file are constantly gazing upon the time clock, like the natives of old would cast supplicating eyes toward the sun and moon. They pray for the clock hands to speed up while they toil at their stations, and then plead again for the hands to slow down while they take their breaks. At quitting time they bolt for the doors, displaying bursts of energy unlike any they have shown all day. For what? Do they have rare tickets to hear Pavarotti? Is a loved one having surgery? Perhaps a son is giving his dissertation? No, they simply want to make sure they get a good stool at the Dew Drop Inn. Once seated, they complain nonstop about working at the plant—until they get laid off, and then they complain about that!

Such contradictions zigzag throughout their thoughts and actions, as I tried to explain to Nicholas during one of our visits to the plant. We paused near the quieter fulfillment section and leaned our forearms on the catwalk railing.

"Let me tell you about the 'lottery phenomenon,' as I like to call it. Whenever the jackpot rises to record levels, the plant floor is abuzz with high-spirited talk of what they'd do if they won. They'd buy a fishing boat, a new car, or a big house. Of course, the first thing they say they'd do is call me on Monday morning, tell me off, and then quit."

"There must be one or two who have talents if given the chance," Nicholas said.

"Oh, I'm not denying they have ingenuity. You should see

some of the stuff security catches them trying to sneak out of here."

"Good thing we don't have to worry about that over by us."

"What? Do you know something?"

"No. Just seems like we go through a lot of office supplies."

"Well, sure we do. We've been busy lately. Anyway, where was I? Oh, yes, contradictions. As much as they don't care for us, it's surprising how much they want to be like us."

"They do?"

"Sure. They want power over others, more money than they know what to do with, and the freedom to come and go as they please. But, what happens when they get it? Ten years later, these lottery winners are lonely, broke, and miserable. The reality is, they aren't suited to being like us. Therefore, we have an obligation to limit their power, ration their financial resources, and provide firm structure in their lives."

"God help them if you weren't here," Nicholas said reverently.

N: *Dark Secret*

I always wondered whether I should have told Hub that I spent time working on an assembly line before I went to college. Maybe I just should have shown up in my cube one day with a chain wallet sticking out of my pants.

H: *Tours*

Actually, a day or two of training in the plant when you are first starting out can be of some value. Such a pilgrimage may win you lifelong admiration from the workers, many of whom will bond with you as "one of them."

As you move up the ladder, however, most of your forays into the plant will occur when you guide visiting executives, investors, and clients through to reassure them that the company at its core is well-oiled and industrious. Be aware that this is also an opportunity to loom large in their eyes as you stand like a general overlooking the strange, booming theater of iron machinery. With each thunderous clang of steel on the assembly line, you swell. When masses of soiled men wearing hardhats obey your commands, your status rises. As each fearsome forklift roars past, your image grows ever larger—for you are one of the masters of this heart of darkness.

"You needn't stand quite so close to me, Miss Emery. The lift drivers have strict instructions to maintain at least a 5-foot distance."

"Oh . . . sorry. The sharp forks frighten me."

"I understand."

When leading an expedition through the labyrinth of gears, bearings, conveyors, vats, and brimstone, pause only for a moment at points of interest, and then move quickly onward. Such sights may sear the consciousness if dwelled upon at length. Keep your breaths short and shallow, lest the sparks in the air and the smell of hot metal choke your lungs. Along the path, as workers steal furtive glances at your group, pay them no heed. If encouraged, they may become emboldened to speak directly to a straggler in your party. Without advance training, there is no telling what inappropriate utterances may proceed from the mouths of your workers. Horror stories abound of line workers letting slip tales of personal mistreatment, alleged safety violations, and inferior manufacturing processes of the long-distant past. Uncouth loading-dock workers will offend your visitors merely by the language they unconsciously use.

"Helluva afternoon, ain't it? Here ta grab the company by the balls are ya?"

"Come again?"

"Ain't you one of them Wall Street tight-asses that's here to buy out the chief?"

"Oh, no, no. I'm on your side. I flew in from the Dallas office."

"Dallas, eh? I got a joke 'bout a gay cowboy? Wanna hear it?"

This is when you'd better be near enough to hustle your straggler along to the next stop.

It is best not to stare at and photograph the workers as though they were zoo inhabitants. Strive instead to avoid eye contact by gazing over their heads or off to the sides, beyond them. Workers treated like invisible objects will learn their place and will cause less trouble. Whenever one happened to call out to me, I pointed first to my ear and then the machinery, waved, and quickly motioned my party onward.

N: *Uprisings*

I guess way back when, before the union came in, there must have been a smart one on the floor somewhere, because Hub's managers kept getting messages in the suggestion box that made more sense than the way they were running things. But the managers didn't do anything, because they didn't want to give credit to some "temp" guy making minimum wage.

Other workers on the floor found out about it though, and soon enough the discontentment started to grow.

"I learned a hard lesson from that episode," Hub confided. "If not squashed immediately, they'll eventually be contacted by a parasitic union organizer who can sniff out the scent of a rebellion, no matter how far away his headquarters are."

H: *The Brotherhood*

I could never in a thousand pages prepare you for dealing with the wiles of *the union*—the shady brotherhood of conspiracy types who could find crop circles in their shag carpeting. Close your eyes and imagine a nondescript building near the railroad tracks in the oldest part of town. Nearby are several taverns and an Elks Club, which pretends to be a restaurant on Fridays and serves cheap battered fish.

Inside the darkness of the union hall you sit on a folding metal chair and try to make out shadowy forms toward the front of the room, countenances lit faintly by the light of cigarettes. They are the ordained missionaries, the ones who do the recruiting work of the Local 1070 outpost. (The high priests serve elsewhere, in more luxurious surroundings.) It is within these dark walls that the secret counts and recounts take place. From here go forth the orders for the sacred stones of rebellion to be offered up at the windows of the capitalist master.

In a corner lean unused picket signs. Fortunately, the union's power is waning. The heathen, now represented by your independent and apathetic generation, are not as easy to convert as in the past. "People don't get involved like they used to," grumbles the union steward as you hurry back outside.

N: *Too Many Collars*

Let's see, there's white collar (office, male), pink collar (office, female), blue collar (factory), gray collar (semi-professional), black collar (church), green collar (agriculture), and ring-around-the-collar. Too many divisions, in my opinion. We all wear T-shirts at my recording studio.

Hub encouraged an anti-union sentiment by holding big parties for management at his 8,236-square foot waterfront mansion, which he called Hearst Castle East. I know the dimensions precisely, because Hub told me at least a dozen times.

"You must have one of these," he greeted me, handing over a drink as I entered the portico. "It's called a Boa Constrictor. It's our traditional drink after we've squeezed another round of concessions out of the union."

"What's in it?"

"Blackberry brandy. Try it."

I did, and told him I liked it, mostly so I could break away and meet up with Janelle, Derek, and Serena. I wandered around inside first—though parts of the 8,236-square foot house were cordoned off—like a mouse following a maze of hallways into rooms with countless framed mirrors, polished candlesticks, gleaming crystal, and stiff Persian rugs. Serena had told me that the board of directors had given Hub a bonus to help finance the place, with the stipulation that he would use it often to entertain clients.

Most of the action appeared to be taking place in the sunken gardens, so I left the 8,236-square foot confines and stepped outside.

"Did you see this place?" exclaimed Derek as I approached. "That's his yacht in the fountain, and there's the lagoon. He's got a tennis green, too—I was on it earlier—and a putting court behind those trees."

"Slow down, Derek, you're not making any sense," I said.

"Can you believe that?" Janelle said.

"Yeah—what's Liza doing here?" I said.

"That's what I mean. Making the secretaries serve as wait-staff!"

Serena interrupted and said something about a budget crunch. "If things don't improve, next time *we'll* be the ones handing out hors d'oeuvres. He's already got some guy from the plant maintaining his cars."

"There's his wife," said Derek, sticking his neck like a giraffe above the crowd.

"How do you spell her name anyway?" Janelle asked.

"Why? Adding her to your Tupperware list?" I said.

Hub, drink in hand, wandered over with Britknee and put his arm on her shoulders like someone puts his arm up on the back of his sofa.

I saw Derek wince ever so enviously. Janelle said hello, and Serena turned partially away.

Another guest interrupted us. "Oh, Brit—your new hairstyle is absolutely fabulous!"

"I know."

Hub had that self-satisfied air about him—as if he had earned all of his good fortune and deserved it as naturally as the air he breathed.

"Have you seen the place yet?" Britney asked. "Come. I'll give you all a tour. Follow along now!"

Rich people create a stir wherever they go. Following us, as we followed Hub and Britney, was an ant-like entourage of guests, busily anticipating some exciting morsel, because the king and queen of the castle hovered near.

I drank too much and stayed later than I had wanted. Even with the benefit of Hub's tour, on the way out I got lost in the 10,236-square foot mansion (I found some additional rooms I'll bet even Hub didn't know existed). It was probably about two o'clock in the morning. I was so disoriented, I must have turned down the same hallway five separate times. Or, maybe they were different hallways—who knows. Suddenly, I heard splashing and laughing. It sounded like Hub! I turned around immediately to escape, only to come flush with another of those confounded mirrors. In the reflection I saw Hub sitting in a hot tub with Liza!

Where was Britney? I wondered as I headed for the front door at last. Hey! There were Janelle and Serena. But, where was Derek?

13

REPORTING & EVALUATIONS

H: *A Brief History*

In the early days, my generation never bothered with formal employee evaluations. My first boss had a stuffed monkey he sat on a cabinet out in the hallway. Occasionally, he would put a dunce cap on the monkey, with the point of the cap aimed at the office of whoever had just screwed up. That was all the evaluation we had time for! We were too busy winning wars and building this country. If somebody wasn't cutting the mustard we took him aside and told him to shape up. We held his feet to the fire, and if there wasn't immediate improvement we showed him the door.

Eventually, as things settled down, we put in place a comprehensive program of procedures; reviews; evaluations; expense accounts; tallies; charts; telephone logs; and daily, weekly, monthly, quarterly, semiannual, and year-end reports. These were carefully filed in rows of folders and cabinets, providing managers with a ready store of information about their employees and various division activities.

Today, many of these records are beginning to be phased out

under hasty paperwork reduction initiatives. Apparently, younger, impatient generations have complained so often about "red tape" that many of the most trusted forms have been reduced, eliminated, or—worse yet—put online.

N: *Paperwork*

"Do we really need these telephone logs from 1972?" I asked Hub one day.

"We might. Why?"

"I had to put two people in one cube to make room for the new filing cabinets that came yesterday. I was thinking maybe we could toss some of these old records and avoid taking up more room with cabinets."

"Well, I suppose. But God help us if the carbon copies in the basement are ever damaged."

"I'll have a sentry posted."

"Go ahead and scoff, but the day you throw them out is the day you'll end up needing them."

"What about these old golfing scorecards?"

"Don't you dare touch those," Hub said, his eyes growing large.

"Oh, I wasn't going to. But some of them look kind of tattered. I thought we might scan and archive them in a database. Then we could load them on a laptop and bring it along to the course. You would have instant access to every score you ever posted on a given hole. In fact, we could run some statistical analysis and compute your mean score and standard deviations. Then you'd have an idea how difficult a hole was for you based on your past performances."

"There, you see—you make fun of *my* paperwork, but *your* crazy databases are ten times worse."

H: *Feedback*

Managers once reviewed employee performance only when there was trouble. Most problems will solve themselves if they are swept under the rug promptly enough. Nowadays, every little paper cut has to be handled with the seriousness of the Cuban missile crisis. To supposedly prevent problems from festering, new employees have demanded touchy-feely "coaching" sessions every six months, where struggling workers are coddled and cajoled to improve their performance, and top performers are endlessly praised.

"All I want is a little feedback," Nicholas sat in front of my desk and told me on his one-year anniversary with the company. "My manager won't give me a review. Probably because he doesn't really understand what I do. Plus, he's hardly ever around."

"Sounds like you have no problem giving *him* a review," I retorted. (Heaven forbid that we ever started down *that* path. Managers reviewed by their subordinates! Such hooey.) "So you want a little feedback?" I continued. "You young people claim to be independent and detached, yet you're forever wanting this feedback stuff." (I guess things are different in the shades-of-gray place that your world has become. It's hard for you to measure yourself without clear values like my generation had.)

"I'd just like to know how I'm doing and where I can improve my performance."

"Fair enough. You can start by spending more time working and less time worrying about how you're doing. You want irony? That 'Just Do It' slogan your generation plasters everywhere refers far more accurately to *my* generation than yours. In my day, we rolled up our sleeves and plunged in. We didn't spend months planning. We didn't worry about consequences. And we didn't need to notify every clown who thought he might be affected. That's how we won World War II. . . ."

"Is that also how you won in Korea and Vietnam?"

"It's how we built bridges and highways . . ."

"That have damaged the countryside with sprawl."

"And how we built billion-dollar corporations."

"That practically killed Lake Erie."

"Now, Nicholas, if you'll excuse me, I've a meeting to prepare for."

"Mr. Ablebright, did you hear a word I said?"

Don't be silly.

H: *Self-Evaluations*

I suppose if everybody these days feels they need an evaluation, the most painless method for a manager involves the self-evaluation form. At least the manager won't have to do anything.

The problem is, the employee filling one out is forced to 1) be honest and condemn himself, 2) fudge his record to protect himself, or 3) look like a braggart if indeed he has been a top performer.

1) **Honesty:** "My performance on the Lindsay project was disappointing by all accounts. Still, thanks to my low salary, one might make a case for keeping me on another year if not for my even more pathetic display at the October board meeting. I've probably said enough already, but I would be less than forthcoming if I didn't mention the $550 of phony charges on my expense reports over the last six months. Self-assessment: I need help."

2) **Fudging:** "My performance on the Lindsay project was hampered by poor organizational support. My team-first attitude makes me a prime candidate to retain another year. Besides sacrificing additional compensation, I sacrificed some of my dignity at the October board meeting so others could shine. Attached you will find my self-audited expense reports. Self-assessment: I'm becoming more valuable every day."

3) **Braggart:** "My performance saving the Lindsay project was outstanding considering the no-win situation I was up against. Even though I am earning 50% less than I could working elsewhere, my effort level remains at its maximum, as was clearly evident during the October board meeting, when I saved the company from certain bankruptcy. I confess my expense reports are grossly inaccurate, since they do not reflect innumerable work-related charges I incurred at my own expense. Self-assessment: I'm one of the top employees in the history of this company, and it's time my heroics were recognized."

I recommend that you choose option three. As any propaganda expert will testify, if something is repeated often enough, eventually people will start to believe it.

H: *Top-Down Evaluations*
If your company does not favor the self-evaluation form, when

you become a manager you will have to fill out evaluations for those reporting to you. These things are confidential, right? You won't be showing them to anyone else, and the employees won't be sharing them with each other. Therefore, what's to prevent you from simply filling out every form exactly the same? This not only saves time and effort, it is quite effective for a number of reasons.

This works best when you mark every item "Needs Improvement." Since no one is perfect, what could be more accurate? There are additional benefits to this strategy. First, it keeps your employees on edge, which makes them more careful about being on time and getting their work done. Second, it limits the movement of star employees to competitors, since you will have them convinced they are not as outstanding as they once believed. Third, it protects you from lawsuits later when pay raises are not forthcoming. And, fourth, this strategy lifts you as a manager, with the power to hire and fire, to the level of sainthood in their eyes for continuing to patiently carry them along.

H: *Enhancing Your Performance Report*
Traditionally, one or two employees are annually scheduled to present reports orally before the brass. Through the grapevine you should be able to learn when your opportunity is scheduled. You must put some effort into these "focus" reports on the off chance that one of the bigwigs at the table might actually stay awake long enough to hear what you're saying.

One of the most effective things you can do to enhance your report is to get on a team that oversees a high-profile project. This is an ideal way to look good without necessarily having to do much. Such an oversight team, while getting the credit for successes, never actually works on the project itself—it just coordinates it. Typically, such a team will meet far more often than it should for far longer than it needs to. Consequently, you can be out of the office from 8 A.M. until 1 P.M. one day every week on what is perceived by everyone to be an important mission.

If you choose the project team wisely, there will be a number of high-profile company leaders sitting on it and an equal number of Eager Beavers anxious to knock themselves out implementing all of the objectives the team proposes. Your best bet is to volunteer to prepare the team's reports. Because this duty is perceived as necessary but unpleasant, no one usually wants this job, so you'll probably have no trouble getting it. In fact, everyone will be grateful to you for volunteering. The best thing is, you'll never have to do another thing on that team but join in the credit for its activities. And, because you're already making what everybody believes to be a big contribution, you'll seldom have to volunteer for anything else.

The best part is, doing the reports is not as terrible as it's made out to be. Reports are seldom looked at afterward and, even then, most people don't remember what really happened. If you make a mistake it will be difficult to prove. Furthermore, it's actually your secretary who does all of the work anyway.

When it comes time to make that focus presentation, you can trot out your trophy: Your accomplishments as an integral part of a respected team working on a well-known project. With pride and confidence you can show slides of the project and proclaim, "*We* completed this award-winning project on time and under budget, and the benefits will accrue for years to come."

N: *Reviewing Reports*

Well, he's right about one thing: Reports are seldom looked at. I'd be willing to bet that in all of the years Hub has been receiving reports, he has probably never read a single one.

"I didn't get that report done for you," I told Hub at the month's end, "because I was too busy reviewing all of the reports from my staff."

"Oh, you don't have to review those. It's not the *substance* of reports that counts, it's the *act* of reporting that's critical. Reporting forces underlings to analyze their performance—and it reinforces the manager-worker hierarchy."

"By the way, what did you think of the issue I raised in my report last month?"

Hub nodded appreciatively and assured me that the issue I raised would be looked at carefully in the near future.

"But we need to act on it quickly," I pressed him, realizing that he was hosing me. "You saw how much money we could save by reengineering our inventorying process."

"These things must proceed through the proper channels," he told me earnestly as he quietly but firmly motioned me out of his office.

I have heard that after I left the company, Hub championed my idea as his own—and the reengineering I suggested made an immediate impact.

H: *Reports That Are Doomed From The Start*

Imagine the reporting predicament you'd be in if the ill-conceived telecommuting trend ever became established. You'd face the near impossible task of trying to convince the top brass that you've been hard at work at home the past year. They'd never buy it, no matter how diligent you might have been. Let's face it, the odds of anyone keeping their nose to the grindstone while working at home are slim to none. There are just too many distractions.

In a rare instance of poor judgment, I once let a female staffer, whom I shall call Miss Bixley, talk me into allowing her to work at home three days per week. Her hiatus came to an abrupt end one morning when I stopped by her home unexpectedly to drop off a report.

I went straight to the back door, where Miss Bixley kept her "office," and was greeted by an older woman blowing on her fingernails.

"Is Miss Bixley in?" I inquired.

"Oh, you must be the accountant," the woman chirped at me. "Come in. She'll be back down shortly. We were right in the middle of my manicure when that little girl she watches got into the caramel apples again."

I stepped inside and nearly tripped over a toy fire truck.

"She's upstairs giving her a bath. She got sticky stuff all over herself."

My gaze turned toward the desk. Beside the pile of papers and the computer monitor I noticed a half-eaten caramel apple sitting threateningly on the mouse pad. Atop the frightened keyboard sat a wild bag of Doritos ready to launch its crumbs.

The woman sat down in one of the two chairs near a table covered with mirrors, scissors, clippers, and other instruments. "I'm one of her original customers," the woman said proudly. "She's doing quite well now. But I'm sure you already know that."

"I'm *not* her accountant—I'm her boss from her *real* job. The job that's supposed to be her *only* job!"

"Oh, dear."

Suddenly there was a bustle in the hallway.

"Can we work on that big jigsaw puzzle now?" a child's voice pleaded.

"Not right now, Jamie. I've got to finish with my customer first."

Miss Bixley, clad in bathrobe and sneakers, turned remarkably pale as she entered the room and spotted me waiting inside. "I won't trouble you with this report," I said coldly. "I can see you're terribly busy. I'd offer to stay and help finish up this lady's nails so you could tackle that puzzle, but I've got to get back and meet with my personnel manager. Seems there's a vacancy on my staff that just opened up."

N: *Multitasking*

I say "Miss Bixley" deserves our admiration for working her butt off to make ends meet. If companies would pay office staff a decent wage, they wouldn't have to juggle three different jobs.

H: *Not Like It Used to Be*

It's not corporate America's fault so many women of marrying age are hellbent on supporting themselves. The wages being paid are meant to be supplementary, not primary.

Things sure have changed. I toss this "working at home" concept right on the heap of artificial realities we've seen blossom in the last few years. Everything has become a weak imitation of what it used to be. Instead of holding a real job in a real office, people start a half-baked business at home. And, on it goes. Instead of recording a real album with a real record company, a band of dropouts make a disc in their garage and form an "indie" label. Rather than publish a real book with a real publishing house, so-called writers self-publish their books and sell through online "bookstores" that don't even have any shelves. Somebody with a video camera who can't get near Hollywood ends up with his own "show" on a cable access station—or worse, his own witch movie in the theater.

I could go on and on. We used to have real beer like Pabst Blue Ribbon, real white sugar, and real baseball with players like Joe DiMaggio. Today we're left with "lite" beer, saccharin, and the All-Star Game ending in a tie. For Pete's sake!

N: *Oh, Really?*

Hub's depth perception is a little foggy. Wasn't it his generation that replaced breast milk with formula, steel with plastic, and cotton with polyester?

If he wants to talk "real" jobs, he ought to go back to the slaughterhouses in Chicago or the farms on the frontier. Now those were real jobs—not sitting in some cozy office conducting meetings all day. If he wants to talk real books, we ought to go back to scrolls, or at the very least, Gutenberg. And, he'd better toss those albums out. The only real music is the kind you hear live, played by orchestras and chamber groups.

14

MEETINGS

N: *Meetings Ad Nauseam*

"Not another meeting," I muttered to Janelle as we met in the hallway.

She rolled her eyes. "I know. This makes *four* this week."

Hub, who must have overheard us, turned around and said, "Don't worry, this will be the last meeting we ever have." Then he and Harry elbowed each other and laughed.

Real funny. Here's a typical week's schedule. In the meeting on Monday they make us review the meetings we had last week. On Tuesday, we have to meet to discuss what our meetings are going to be about *this* week. On Wednesday, we meet all afternoon on an issue before finally deciding we need additional information before we can take action. Another meeting is then scheduled for Friday morning.

H: *No Agenda Is Best*

Wait a minute! Who canceled the Thursday meeting?

Self-proclaimed management consultants, who have no idea what meetings are really all about, sponsor overly serious seminars on running meetings. They stress the need for clear, specific agendas and firm leadership in sticking to them. Poppycock. Shareholder meetings are best served by vague, dull agendas to discourage anybody from attending, and client and in-house meetings need no agenda at all.

Though I do not share your generation's distaste for formal meetings, I at least partly agree with your tendency to prefer spontaneity. In strategic meetings true leadership is off-the-cuff and free-flowing. Specific agendas only encourage over-preparation and rehearsed dialogue. Anyone can be persuasive or underhanded when they've had days to prepare for an encounter. The question is, how do they *really* feel about the merger or the overseas expansion? The only way to find out is by asking them out of the blue, when they're not expecting it.

That's when alliances are formed on the fly, promises are made that otherwise wouldn't be, and gut-level decisions are blurted out—which is how things get done. What can you do to prepare? Probably nothing—I am simply warning you ahead of time, so that when a moment arises like the one below, you are not knocked off stride by a meeting that refuses to follow the agenda you were expecting.

"Well, gentlemen," I would begin, puffing my cigar with a dramatic air, "I know you thought the company was doing well, (puff) but the truth is we're going to have to eliminate one of your departments (puff) by the end of the day (puff, puff)."

Blank stares and silence.

"Hassenfuss," I continue, pointing my stogie at the bean counter across from me, "who do you think it should be? You?"

With no time to prepare alliances against me or to bamboozle others with trumped-up figures showing the supposed indispensability of each department, he has no choice but to blurt out the name of the least profitable division. Like sharks the others quickly join the feeding frenzy. In five minutes we have initiated and finalized a decision that I have watched others stretch into months of fiscal impact studies and tedious negotiations.

N: *Confidentiality*

I have seen executives play a game in meetings called "The Confidence

Game." This is where a VP dismisses the secretary, leans forward across the conference table, and in a serious tone announces that what he is about to share with the group is to be kept confidential. The group is usually flattered to be taken into the VP's select circle of trust.

Then, after spilling something juicy, he lets the same secret slip later that day to the person he considers the office's Gadabout Parrot. The news eventually gets out, but no one realizes that the VP was the guilty party, because once a message is in the grapevine it's almost impossible to trace.

This has the effect of creating an atmosphere of uneasiness in the next meeting, which significantly increases the VP's power and provides a great opportunity to recruit support for just about any pet proposal. Since the group is convinced they have let the VP down, the only option is to try to make it up to him.

N: *The Ominous Note*

Though not as effective as "The Confidence Game," the results of the "Ominous Note Ploy" are more immediate. I have seen executives use it when they expect to find themselves in a battle with one of the division heads.

Apparently, they leave a folded note in a sealed envelope with a secretary before they go into the meeting, and they instruct her to bring it in to them about ten minutes after the meeting has started. This interruption, of course, grabs everybody's attention. The VP immediately opens the envelope, lets his face grow serious as he pretends to read it, then looks up ominously at his rival. He continues reading and looking up at his rival two or three more times. Then he carefully refolds the letter, puts it back in the envelope, and quickly places it in his jacket pocket. By now the rival has probably grown pale—or at least he is too distracted to be on top of his game—and the VP will have gained a big mental advantage.

H: *Meeting Notes*

The young have vivid imaginations! I have never seen either of the tactics Nicholas describes. Perhaps if he were doing something useful at meetings, like taking notes, he wouldn't have time to daydream.

Whether as a junior member of the group you have the opportunity to take notes or your secretary does, the minutes are an opportunity for you to further your objectives. However, it takes subtlety and experience to carry it off successfully. You must learn to manage your emotions and judgments. You might *want* the minutes to include something like, "Then that jackass Fred Jones, VP of logistics, made a totally inaccurate and asinine comment about my Tellar Project, of which he knew practically nothing." But, you must remain in control when writing the minutes or editing your secretary's notes.

There is nothing wrong with slanting the proceedings to promote your point of view or cleverly editorializing to make someone else look bad, but if you're caught it will mean tape recording all meetings in the future, and no one wants that kind of accountability.

The key in successful note taking is not to put words in people's mouths or reinterpret what they say—*it is in knowing what to leave out.* In the example above, I would have ignored Jones' negative comment entirely. Other execs reading a recap of the meeting in the days afterward would therefore never see that a VP was against your project. Even better, you can actually use Jones' comment to your benefit. Most likely, someone else, like Jim Smith in marketing, will have spoken up in defense of the project along the lines of, "Well, Fred, I agree that the project's a loser, but don't forget that it's opened up some doors for us."

Rather than recording both quotes or even a summary like, "Managers spoke both for and against the Tellar project," you can simply write, "Jim Smith, VP of marketing, told the group that the Tellar Project has 'opened up some doors for us.'"

Manipulating *context* is also an excellent way to tilt momentum against your opponents. Let's pick on VP Jones again (why not, the guy's a jerk). Let's say no one had said anything following his comment about the Tellar Project, either for or against it. You could isolate Jones by writing, "Fred Jones, VP of logistics, was the only one to say anything against the Tellar Project." Without the proper context, later readers would think Jones was bellyaching about a project that everyone else was happy with.

H: *Meeting Spoilers*
When I ran a meeting I expected full attention. I have seen all of the tricks in my day and so have most veteran executives. Do not

think as Nicholas once did that you can fold *The Onion* into your copy of the company's annual report and get away with sitting there all afternoon reading about the Pope converting to Islam or some other such nonsense.

Whether it's a board meeting, a staff meeting, or a meeting with clients, several of the traits found in the "Office Characters" chapter often show up around the table. Make sure you don't fall into these habits. The proper response, of course, will vary depending on your status (Me = executive level; You = junior manager).

- **Ladder Climber Monkey:** Brings piles of documents with him and uses the time in your meetings to get his regular work done.
  Me: I would loudly remark that if he were more efficient like the rest of the group, he might not have to bring his work with him all the time.
  You: Since Monkey is openly saying his work is more important than you are, call for his opinion constantly to disturb him as often as possible.

- **Double-Jobber Ant:** Continually answering his cell phone or being called out of the meeting.
  Me: "Give me your phone."
  "Why?"
  "Because the next call that comes in, *I'm* answering it."
  You: "Could you turn vibrate on instead of the ringer?"

- **Kindergartner Fawn:** Will take ten minutes describing a totally impractical proposal.
  Me: I made sure the record reflected that my rivals supported every word of it.
  You: Nod politely when she finishes and say you'll consider it at the next meeting.

- **Handwringer Chihuahua:** Afraid to vote yea or nay on anything, even adjournment.
  Me: When the secretary tallied the votes on a proposal, I would jump in and insist that Chihuahua had voted with me. (He never denied it.)

You: Offer that you believe Chihuahua actually meant to abstain.

- **Nonconformist Cat:** Will object to even the most innocent of proposals. Takes perverse joy in making certain that no board vote is unanimous.
  Me: I avoided the situation altogether by having my secretary send Cat an agenda with the wrong date and/or room number. (He probably enjoyed holding his own private meeting anyway.)
  You: He's usually in the minority, so don't worry about him too much.

- **Oblivious Olive:** She knows she's at a table but is aware of little else. Don't be surprised if you startle her and she responds, "Hit me!" or "I'll have the surf-and-turf."
  Me: I simply marked her absent.
  You: You could toss her a face card and an ace, but she probably wouldn't realize the significance. Or, you could ask her what she'll have for dessert—who knows, she might leave you a tip.

- **Easily Offended Horse:** A low-volume client who walks out of the meeting because you won't give him the same discounts that you give your long-standing, high-volume clients.
  Me: A client like this one creates more trouble than he's worth. I would announce that the figure I quoted him was indeed wrong—then declare that because his company was such a small player, I was going to have to add an additional surcharge to all of his shipments.
  You: Since you probably need every client you can get, you'd better corral him and offer him at least a small discount.

- **Hypochondriac Guinea Pig:** Coughs, sneezes, and wheezes throughout the meeting. May even fall off her chair and injure her back.

Me: Sat as far away as possible.
You: Offer her a cough drop.

- **Babbler-With-A-Cause Turkey:** Can't make a single point without first going off in a dozen different directions that have little or nothing to do with the subject at hand. (Actually, this is perfectly normal at meetings, so don't worry about it.)

N: *Purpose Of Meetings*

Most of the meetings I sat through at Hub's company seemed to be for the purpose of micromanaging employees. At my studio, meetings are scheduled sparingly, and then mostly to share ideas and work together. Everyone is empowered to jump in and participate.

H: *American Civics Lesson*

Don't get me started on "empowerment." We have never lived in a democracy. We live in a republic. Big difference. In their wisdom the founding fathers decided it was better to be led by the corrupt few than the incompetent many.

N: *Classical Greek Civics Lesson*

The only way the "incompetent many" are going to become competent is by taking the reins.

15

SPEAKING AT SEMINARS

H: *Oratory*

In 1999, Frenchman Lluis Colet broke U.S. Senator Strom Thurmond's world record by speaking to an audience non-stop for twenty-four hours and twenty-one minutes, aided only by occasional sips of wine. Oratory such as this was more common in the industrious days of the early 20th century, when employees and citizens were eager to gain instruction at the feet of their leaders.

As an unknown newcomer to the world of business, one of the fastest ways you can make your mark is by the power of your oral communication skills in meetings and at seminar presentations. Unfortunately, the weak or non-existent speech training you received at college has undoubtedly left you prepared only to showcase your awkwardness. I suggest you rush post-haste to your nearest Toastmasters Club, and beg them to include you in their program. Even then it will take you some time to gain polish and confidence, but once you do you will be ready to step toward greatness if you follow these admonitions.

H: _You Are The Most Important Part Of A Seminar, Not The Audience_

With this fundamental attitude always in mind, you will have the confidence to stride up to that podium and tell the audience every last thing you know about a particular subject. You will possess the steel to turn what could have been a half-hour presentation into a two-hour discourse. (I know your generation is up to it—Nicholas showed me a Weblog once.)

It takes resolve to stand in front of an audience for hours, marching steadily through your material, as audience members unfit for the challenge gradually retreat from the building. Remember always that without your presence, there would be no seminar.

N: _Near Record_

"Wow, Mr. Ablebright, for a while there I thought you were going to break that French guy's record," I said after the first time I heard Hub speak. "Too bad so many people left."

"If need be, a noble speaker can carry on without a single audience member remaining," Hub declared.

He should know!

H: _Bios_

To help with their introductions, conference and seminar organizers will usually request a brief biography (bio) from you a few days prior to your speaking engagement. I kept a copy of a well-crafted bio in my file for ready distribution. I would offer it to you as a model, but I fear your inability to match it would only discourage you. Then again, you must be shown the stars if you are to reach for them. One key to an effective bio is to build your credibility—and if you also create a bit of awe in your audience, that can only help your cause. The other key is to emphasize all three of the sacred triumvirate: Power, money, and sex.

> BIO FOR HENRY "HUB" ABLEBRIGHT
> Dr. Ablebright is currently the founder and Chief Executive Officer of Ablebright Manufacturing Corporation and has been a senior executive for

over twenty years at three Fortune 500 corporations, all of which have fallen out of the ranking since his departure. He has personally authored too many books and articles to mention here and is a veteran speaker on the conference circuit. His wife is a former Junior Miss Pennsylvania and has won numerous gymnastics and wet T-shirt titles. He sponsors a thoroughbred racing team and once owned a rare Cadillac. In high school he was an all-conference wrestling champion and invented a stunning "double takedown" move still talked about in hushed tones today. He is also an honorary fellow.

Technically, I did not have a doctorate degree (though I considered my experience to be equivalent). Nevertheless, I added it to my biography because I was quite sure that once the audience heard my presentation they would be *more* incredulous to find I did *not* have such a degree. And remember, credibility is critical. (I am not sure exactly when I became an honorary fellow, but I assume I must have become one somewhere along the way.)

N: *Credentials*

So, Hub really isn't a doctor. He sure had me fooled.

H: *Make Sure You Are The Only One There With A Working Microphone*

There was an idyllic time when audience members were content to sit quietly and listen. Now interactive sessions are often forced upon seminar speakers. And we know there's nothing worse than some speaker wannabe from the audience stealing precious moments from our monologues with their self-serving reflections. It's much easier to talk over these chatty audience members when *we* have microphones and *they* don't.

However, you can be clever and fool the audience into thinking that their input is sought (though we know darn well it isn't) by setting up a lectern and microphone off to the side of the seating.

Now here's the good part: Make sure beforehand to pack the chairs and rows tightly. Few people will go to the inconvenience of excusing their way through the crowded chairs to get to the lectern. As an additional precaution, the quality of the mike should be so poor that anyone daring to use it will sound like a cross between Donald Duck and the Cheshire Cat, fading in and out between scratchy syllables. I have seen this setup work beautifully at several public input sessions.

N: *Turning The Tables*

The city plan commission tried a similar arrangement one time for a hearing involving a major project in the neighborhood where my loft was located. I don't usually bother with such meetings, because the public servants seem to have their minds made up already, but a bunch of us were looking to get rowdy that night, so we went. The room was set up just like Hub described, but it didn't matter to us, because Gonzo (one of my friends) brought along a Mr. Microphone he had snarfed from his little sister, who used to pretend she was J. Lo.

Hardly anyone in the audience said anything at first, because they saw how difficult it was to get to the lectern. Even when someone on the outside of the rows went, they were discouraged by the poor mike quality. Then Gonzo stood up with our mike and gave a hellacious speech. After that we started passing our mike all over the room, and people who probably wouldn't have said anything that night were spilling their guts. The head commissioner gave Gonzo the dirtiest look afterward. We still laugh about it!

H: *Adjust Your Style Only When It Serves You*

It is best to stick with one speaking style for all audiences and force *them* to adapt, especially when you are an inexperienced speaker. Nevertheless, there may be unusual circumstances when you voluntarily decide to adjust your style. This is acceptable if done for the right reasons.

Example: One of my long-time associates, Dr. Jeffrey Rimplo (who is part of a circle of luminaries you might someday be lucky enough to join), grew tired of people challenging aspects of his messages, so he abandoned his traditional style, in which he always spoke clearly, for a more suitable approach.

"I now turn my head slightly away from the audience at the end of each sentence," he told me, "and let my words trail off into a non-recognizable mumble." This prevents the audience from pinning him down afterward with awkward questions, since they can never be sure just exactly how he ended his point. It's a technique I recommend for just aboun mnymun.

N: *Styling*

I have my own take on adjusting your style. As an audience member, I frequently adjust my style of *listening*, depending on the speaker. If the speaker is especially lame, I will turn my head slightly away from the speaker at the beginning of each sentence and cover my ears with my hands.

H: *If Your Vocabulary Is Ubiquitous, By All Means Showcase It*

By vocabulary I do not mean the crude slang and grunts that formed the core of communication around your college fraternity. I mean, rather, the rich verbiage that you typically "borrowed" from encyclopedias for your term papers. Since most audiences are impressed by words they don't understand, use whatever you can muster, even if it may be out of context.

H: *Foster An Atmosphere Of Discipline And Attention*

This is becoming a difficult task as conference organizers continue to allow ever greater liberties to ensure the comfort and convenience of attendees. I shall comment briefly on some of these abominations.

Plush audience seating. The ancient Greeks were content to sit on rocks while listening to their teachers. Therefore, I always insisted on folding metal chairs to keep my audiences alert.

Breakfast, lunch, and/or dinner provided. Let them eat breakfast before they arrive and dinner after they leave. In the meantime, they can skip lunch. Chances are they do it at work all the time, so why should they change simply because they're attending a seminar?

Cell phones allowed inside. Cell phones should be treated like weapons and confiscated at the entrance. You'd think that with all that's been mentioned about proper phone etiquette, and with all the dirty looks directed toward the offending parties, people would wise up. But it never fails. Every seminar session will be interrupted by at least one dolt's cell phone ringing . . . and ringing . . . and ringing.

> 1st ring: No response from the daydreaming phone owner.
> 2nd ring: Phone owner finally realizes it's *her* phone ringing.
> 3rd ring: She looks in her satchel.
> 4th ring: She searches through her purse.
> 5th ring: She finds the phone in her jacket pocket.
> 6th ring: She checks the display to see who's calling.
> 7th ring: She finally answers the damn thing.

Conference folders. People don't feel the need to listen and take notes, because everything is in the folder. I detected many conventioneers paging through their folders during my presentations, double-checking the time for the next break or meal. Or, perhaps they wanted to know when the brewery tour was leaving after the day's final session. I wish the organizers would include among the materials a bright yellow sheet emblazoned with the words "PAY ATTENTION TO YOUR DAMN SPEAKER!"

N: *Real Discomfort*

C'mon, Hub, let's take this seriously. Why have chairs at all? The audience could sit on sharpened poles instead.

H: *Convict The Audience Of Their Ignorance*

Having heard Nicholas speak, I'm not sure which an audience would find more painful—him or the poles.

But I digress. The stupider an audience believes itself to be, the more likely it will appreciate your instruction. This is especially critical when you are first starting out as a speaker and are barely serviceable yourself. A cunning strategy to achieve this mastery without appearing to be obnoxious involves posing the right type of questions to an unsuspecting audience. While we normally frown on audience participation, there are times when we can use it against them.

The key is to make your questions so difficult that no one can answer them. Ideally, a question will have three or four possible answers, two of which are easy. Of course you magnanimously supply the two easy answers up front, just to show everyone how reasonable the question is. Then you can call on audience members at random, and watch them frantically try to avoid the ensuing silence. Once convicted of their ignorance they will be ever grateful for your patient instruction. (If this sounds familiar, it is probably because one of your professors used this technique on *you*.)

N: *Doh!*
Dem professirs mightta dun dat—I too stupid ta 'member.

H: *Secure The Doors Until Your Presentation Ends*
Yes, it is possible to curtail the popular "anything goes" mentality that ordinarily allows audience members to leave the room early. Though actually locking the doors violates fire codes, you can cleverly arrange for some of your associates to block the exits with their chairs or briefcases.

N: *No Exceptions*
I can personally testify to how well blocking the doors can work. A pregnant woman who claimed she was not allowed to leave the room (Hub swore she was faking it) gave birth in the back row at a seminar he presided over in Winnipeg last year. In a conciliatory gesture, Hub had me mail her another set of handouts from his presentation in case she had missed anything in all of the commotion. (Plus, her original set had been hastily shredded for use as bedding to warm the baby in the frigid conference room.)

H: *Omit Break Periods From The Agenda And Pretend Not To Notice*
The worst thing about breaks is that they kill a presentation's momentum. You spend two solid hours patiently lecturing the

audience, circling around the points like a matador, slowly building up to your first insight—when suddenly the clock reaches some preordained time and the audience bolts for the halls.

When breaks were first introduced into my presentations they were somewhat acceptable five-minute periods that allowed audience members to sharpen their pencils. Soon, as food, drink, and wantonness began to multiply in the hallways, standards slipped, and the period expanded to ten minutes. Currently, the rage is fifteen minutes. Further, by the time today's audiences, undisciplined as they are, return to their seats, an additional five minutes is lost. Carried to its ultimate conclusion, the day approaches when a typical seminar will be five minutes of instruction surrounded by three hours of breaks.

N: *Breaks, Part Two*
Now attendees use the precious break time during Hub's lengthy presentations to phone loved ones who have filed missing persons reports.

H: *Don't Waste Time Trying To Understand Or Relate To Your Audience*
There are some modern speakers who believe they are most effective when they consider the needs of their audiences. What malarkey! If you fall for this psychological drivel, you will end up doing intricate research before presentations to find out precisely what your audiences are hoping to learn. Under the charity of more fully understanding the history and background of a situation, you may even feel compelled to phone the event organizers or people you know who are planning to attend. You must not get caught in this trap!

On a related note, be aware of event organizers who, having their attendees supposedly in mind, boldly send you recommended topics or questions they expect to be addressed in your presentation. Put these presumptuous individuals in their places! Do fans send the quarterback of the football team a list of plays to run? Do concertgoers mandate what songs the conductor plays? Of course not. Making a presentation is substantially an athletic and artistic endeavor. A speaker must be free to follow the inspiration of the moment, wherever it may lead him.

N: *Use Presentation Software To Its Fullest Capacity*

Hub preferred to captivate the audience with the power of his voice and ideas alone, so I was seldom able to persuade him to use presentation software. When he did use it, he certainly got his money's worth. When he found out that somebody once broke a world record by writing the *Declaration of Independence* on a piece of paper the size of a postage stamp, he quickly made his secretary squeeze an entire five-page report on one standard PowerPoint slide. The audience could then study the report using the handout he supplied, read the report on the screen, *and* listen to him read the report to them word for word.

"*That's* how you make a memorable impression," Hub proclaimed proudly.

I tried to tell him that most presentation software supports photos and graphics, too.

Hub remained unconvinced. "I've yet to see any at the seminars I've attended, so that's probably just a rumor," he said. "Why would anybody want to clutter presentations with all of that stuff anyway?" he muttered. "People need to use their imaginations more."

"Good point. I'm going to pantomime my presentations from now on," I responded.

"I did that one time when I had laryngitis. People hung on my every expression."

H: *Live Performances*

Those of you who are interested in further insights will have to attend one of my lectures and study how I handle an audience. I would advise no delay in such attendance, however, for my speaking opportunities are not as frequent as they once were.

16

COMPENSATION

H: *Pay Rates*

Is anything more misunderstood? Executives have received a lot of attention lately for the size of their packages. The two major beefs are 1) executive salaries don't always match company performance, and 2) executive pay rates have risen at a much faster pace than rates for lesser employees.

I must plead ignorance on the first point, since I have no idea within a million either way what my annual salary is. The accountants take care of all that. I have direct deposit at the bank, so I never see a check. All my bills are paid automatically. I just stop by the bank when I need a little spending money, and the manager quietly escorts me into the back and gives me the same size stack each time. When someone asks me how much money I have, I simply answer, "Enough."

Even if I did know what my salary was, I would have no way of knowing how it compared to company performance. The accountants take care of all that. I sign off on something near the end of the summer, but I am very careful not to examine the documents. I made the mistake of looking at the numbers my first year at the helm and was delighted to see no "minuses." I immediately commissioned an architect to design a new office building. The head bean counter was at my desk in no time looking as animated as a bean counter can. When I found out a "parenthesis," of all things, was how they showed a loss, I made up my mind right then and there that I wanted no more part of it.

The less accounting you have to deal with, the better. I've always hired a single firm to perform both the external and internal auditing. Some worrywarts claim this is a conflict of interest. Bosh! I have exactly the same interest in both instances.

Regarding the second point, at first glance executive rates *do* appear to be rising at a faster pace. For example, one study showed executive salaries rising 570 percent over the period 1990 to 2000, while salaries for other employees averaged only a 30 percent increase. However, another study done by the respected Association of American Superiors showed that in the period 1890 to 1900 the "take" of industrialists, railroad barons, and oilmen rose 800 percent. Viewed in its proper historical perspective, today's executive pay rates are rising *far more slowly* than in the past.

Therefore, when the day comes that you, through years of networking, finally reach a level commensurate with an executive compensation package, don't let anyone take you to the woodshed over it. Even if you've led your company into temporary insolvency, you deserve a generous severance package simply for keeping the sinking ship afloat as long as you did.

N: *Okaaay . . .*
It's hard to argue against statistics like those.

H: *The Pie*
It has always been accepted that the world's resources were limited. Pictured like a pie, there were only so many pieces to go around. If I took another piece, then somebody else would have to

settle for less. Now your generation can take heart. There's a breakthrough theory of economics that suggests the world's resources are *not* limited after all. The new assumption holds that the pie is capable of expanding. Thus, if I take more, you not only may keep what you have, you still have every opportunity to gain more for yourself. Understanding this advanced concept silences once and for all that barely audible but nagging voice that tells you to be moderate and restrain yourself. It's just like in the buffet line: Go ahead, reach across, and take *two* pieces—somebody will be along shortly to freshen up the supply.

As your income increases, do not be bothered by the Ms. Envy Hyena and Complainer Crow types who make sour grapes remarks like, "When is enough enough?"—as though amassing it were a crime. Remember, the worst misdeeds are committed not by the fat, but by the starving.

What these critics do not understand is, this is how we keep score. After a certain point it is not about the money any more. It is about striving for excellence in our chosen fields. Our "points" and "victories" happen to have dollar signs in front of them. No one bellyaches that Jack Nicklaus has won more major tournaments than any player in PGA history—in fact, people celebrate his accomplishments. Yet, when an executive "outscores" his rivals, he is attacked rather than honored.

The hypocrisy of the self-righteous "executive whistle-blowers" never ceases to amaze me. They are like the environmentalists who drive gasoline-powered automobiles to their workshops and the animal rights kooks who drive to their protest rallies knowing full well they risk running over a squirrel. The same ones who point fingers at CEOs would trade places in a minute. As Twain said, "I am opposed to millionaires, but it would be dangerous to offer me the position."

N: *"Flaunting"*

Even though I didn't have much experience, because I had an MBA and was hired as management I was given a salary and benefits substantially beyond what non-management employees in the office received. I was able to buy a new car, and Hub insisted on assigning me a parking spot near the front of the building. I wondered whether the other employees would perceive this as flaunting my good fortune.

"Whether it is or not depends entirely on attitude," Hub explained to me. He held up a book and said, "In my dictionary 'flaunting' is carrying on in front of others for no good reason than to make yourself look good."

"So if you 'carry on' about your success for the right reason, it's okay?" I asked.

"At the executive level such carrying on has a higher purpose. When I circle the parking lot for the third time with the top down on my newly waxed Roadster, pretending to search for a parking spot, it's not about *me*. I am simply trying to inspire lesser folks by showing them a goal to strive for. I am saying, 'If you truly commit yourself—pay your dues and have the right connections like I did—you will have a chance to obtain rewards like this rare vehicle or the six-car garage I park it in.'"

"I think I get it now," I said, straining to keep a straight face.

"Don't be too hasty. Believe it or not, flaunting is most often attempted at your pre-executive level where insecure nobodies are trying to impress people like me."

"Well, you can hardly blame them for that."

Hub smiled appreciatively and held up a book again. "'For without vision the people perish,' says the Good Book. Somebody who's made it to the mountaintop must provide others with that vision. Just ask yourself— how many Olympic gold medallists have said watching the ceremonies when they were kids inspired them? Thank heavens some do-gooder hadn't come along and banned the ceremony because the winners were 'flaunting' their hard-won medals."

"I usually need hand puppets to understand stuff, but you have a talent for making everything so clear."

"Although, in light of how liberally they're handing out medals lately, perhaps that wasn't the best analogy. My grandson took home a soccer trophy just for showing up—everybody got one. In my day you had to earn it. And if you didn't earn it, you took your loss like a man and moved on. Nowadays everybody appeals the result or asks for a recount. You didn't see Dewey or Nixon ask for a recount, did you? The only time you need a recount is when a Democrat loses an election for village idiot."

N: *No Difference*
Democrat or Republican—they're all the same to me.

H: *Reaganomics*
The same?! Remember that when those tax-and-spend Democrats are taking another huge bite out of your latest salary increase.

Unfortunately, you're too young to remember the 1980s. That's when a young executive could really make something of himself. And, Americans appreciated and supported it. The ol' Gipper won his second term in a landslide.

N: *The Thing About Landslides*
Landslide victories are generally a disaster for those left standing at the bottom.

H: *More On Trophies*
On a more positive note, many executives are surprised to find that an attractive new wife is often part of the standard compensation package (and the Democrats can't tax *her!*). Of course, this is never formally spelled out in any of the contracts, but many seasoned executives have come to expect it nonetheless.

In my own case, I'm sure my first wife, Millicent, was relieved when the private detective she'd hired brought her the video. She moved out and filed for divorce the next day. The children were grown up by then, so we had no more concerns in that regard. She received a tidy settlement and could finally withdraw from the exhausting schedule that came with being a top executive's wife. By setting her free I gave her a chance at the happiness she always sought but never had time for.

I groomed my new wife, Brittney, from the moment I hired her as an entry-level secretary. I expanded her cultural horizons by insisting that she accompany me on business trips overseas, made sure the company's insurance covered her augmentation surgery, and watched over her progress as she advanced quickly to the rank of executive assistant. Everybody who knows the two of us says we make a stunning couple. In the meantime, of course, I had to hire a new entry-level secretary. I hope she works out.

N: *Turn-About*
You should have seen the look on Hub's face when I told him I was taking Millicent to the movies.

H: *Perks*

Most executive trainees fresh out of school expect nice perks, but even they are often surprised by how generous some companies can be. They may even fret about how it looks when they're awarded fringe benefits that regular company employees worked decades to get. The good thing is, most of them seem to get over it fairly quickly.

Just to be sure you don't settle for too little, I've included a handy guide that you can use to gauge how well your company is meeting its responsibilities.

STANDBY: At your one-year anniversary you get a pen that shows a stripper undressing when you hold it upside down.

COACH: The company pays the charges for mature videos rented during your stay at a conference hotel.

FIRST CLASS: When you treat clients to dinner at Hooters, the company picks up the tab.

PRIVATE JET: The company invests in a corporate membership at a strip club and often holds high-level meetings there, to which you receive regular invitations.

STANDBY: The company supplies screen savers for your computer featuring modern art reproductions.

COACH: Your boss lets you use an old picture frame you scrounged from the storage closet to display a print you bought for your office.

FIRST CLASS: Your office supply budget can be used for new Ansel Adams prints *and* season tickets to the theater.

PRIVATE JET: The company flies your derriere to Paris to pick out a new Renoir for your office, and the CEO wonders why you only bought one, so he sends you back for another.

STANDBY: You get a copy of the company's "PR" video when you're hired.

COACH: The CEO gives a speech, and you get a new calendar showing the regional offices and a coffee mug with a slogan on it.

FIRST CLASS: The company caters lunch and brings in a well-known national speaker. Several top performers, including you, win an all expenses paid round trip to the Bahamas with five-star accommodations.

PRIVATE JET: The company owns a $10-million villa in Puerto Vallarta that needs looking in on regularly, so it sends you whenever you need a blow.

N: *One More*

Actually, Hub forgot one.

STANDBY: You receive a new blanket when you join the company credit union.

COACH: You get a crack at purchasing new stock options before the public does.

FIRST CLASS: The company automatically matches your cash bonuses with the same value in preferred stock.

PRIVATE JET: The company lets you cash out all of your stock options a month before the bankruptcy rumors fly and the bottom drops out.

H: *Putting Up With Ingratitude*

Read the following words carefully. One thing that has rankled me as much as anything over the years is the employee ingratitude I've witnessed at various executive retirement functions. These executives, with little thought for their own comfort or future, have dedicated their entire lives to building their companies and providing paychecks for employees. Then, at what ought to be an opportunity to look back in celebration and appreciation, many employees either don't show up at all, or they arrive empty-handed, prepared only to stuff their mouths with free drinks and appetizers.

Oh, the hat has been passed around the office and many employees have begrudgingly tossed in pocket change, believing this has fulfilled their obligation. How rare is the thoughtful employee who arrives with a separate gift in hand.

My friend, Edmund, who retired last month, was not so lucky. Ed was innocently expecting a new set of Mizuno irons and leather golf bag. He had all he could do to remain gracious when the best gift he received was a duck decoy.

H: *Staff Compensation*

Numerous surveys quote employees from today's younger generations as declaring their job satisfaction can't be "bought" with pay raises. Instead, you and your co-workers champion intangibles such as "opportunities for advancement," "feelings of empowerment," and "challenging assignments" as the qualities that determine whether a job is satisfying.

Having learned the hard way, I finally took employees at their word and kept salary increases to a minimum. I recall giving substantial raises to some of my employees several years ago. They reacted with the expected smiles of surprise and gratitude at first, but within a week their attitudes were scraping bottom once again, proving indeed that money made no difference.

I admit I was confounded. "What's the matter with you sourpusses?" I questioned them. Besides the money, my company offered plenty of challenging assignments and opportunities for advancement, yet these employees remained gloomy. (I figured that by definition it was up to them to supply their own feelings of empowerment.) Since they "had it all"—a great work environment *and* hefty salaries—and still weren't happy, I figured I might as well save the company money by keeping future raises to a bare minimum.

N: *Downsizing*

The office was buzzing when I came in one Monday last summer. One of Hub's Complainer Crows was in rare form, and everyone else was following her lead. Several pink slips had been handed out late Friday, and the remaining employees were being directed to take up the slack. It wasn't long before I found out how much more work I was going to be expected to do. A bunch of us went straight to Hub's office. He looked surprised to see us.

"Mr. Ablebright, we'd like to talk about our new responsibilities," I said as we crowded into the room.

"What's the problem?" he responded evenly.

"Well, we're all swamped already. We think it's only fair that if we're going to be given way more responsibilities, we ought to receive something in return."

"Fine, then," Hub said a bit sternly. "Nicholas, I'll promote you to *senior* assistant division manager and give you an extra three days vacation. Oh, and here's a nice coffee mug I never use."

At this point, most of the older employees resigned themselves to their fate and backed out into the hallway.

"But you already gave me that title two months ago," I said. "And as far as the vacation goes, I'll probably be too busy to use it anyway."

"Let me tell you something," Hub responded, rising behind his desk and increasing the volume of his voice. "It's about time you started thinking about others for a change. Do you think you're the only one who's been given more responsibility? Am I not the head of this company? Doesn't that mean that since *you* now have more responsibility, *I* do too? Well, I can tell you in all certainty that there's been no promotion or monetary increase coming across *this* desk," he barked as he pounded his desktop.

There didn't seem to be much point in continuing the discussion. Hub had already tried the other two standard responses to difficult economic circumstances: 1) raise prices, and 2) use cheaper, less quality materials. That left only the third standard option: Employee layoffs. Well, there is a fourth option, but it's so extreme. I hesitate even to mention it. What you do is re-examine everything you do as a company and look for inefficiencies, waste, and better ways to get the job done. Problem is, that takes effort, analysis, and creativity.

H: *Free Agents*

In the past, employees showed more loyalty than they do now. When you hired somebody, you could count on him settling into his office for several decades. Now many of you have the nerve to sit right at your desks and search for jobs on the Internet or page through the want ads in the break room.

Sooner or later, somebody would saunter into my office, feign sorrow, and announce that he had received an offer from XYZ Corporation for $30,000 more per year than I was paying him. Then he would remark magnanimously that he really liked it here and would hate to leave, and in fact, he'd even consider staying for only $25,000 more. At this point I think this clod honestly believed I would drop to my knees, clasp my hands, and start blubbering in ecstasy that there was a chance to keep him.

I did not fall for such schemes. Depending on the circumstances, I used one of two strategies to turn what would have been a loss for a less resourceful executive into a win-win situation (I win once, and then I win again).

If . . .

1) There was no signed offer on the table, only a gentlemen's agreement.

I pumped Gadabout Parrot for the name of the competing company. Then, I promptly phoned the company and told them it was in their best interest to withdraw their offer. If they did so, I would fire the employee immediately and they could then hire him off the street for the same salary I was currently paying him, which he would be grateful to accept. (As for the $30,000 I saved them, our companies split it.)

Or . . .

2) There was a signed, binding offer on the table.

Usually there was a deadline on the offer, typically thirty days. I would stun the employee by agreeing to match the offer, which resulted in him turning down the competing company. I would then phone the competitor to let them know their prize would be available again after I laid him off thirty days later. They would then be able to hire him at the pre-raise salary he was getting from me. In exchange I asked only that we split the $30,000 that I was saving them.

In the end I was paid $15,000 for getting rid of a disloyal, cancerous employee who had been itching to leave anyway.

N: *Reverse Severance Pay*
Now I know why Hub was so dilated when I left: He didn't make any money off of me.

17

PARTIES

H: *Why Party?*

I once stopped at Nicholas' work area before I left for a long weekend. I wanted to test my theory that every new generation believes it is the greatest "party" generation that ever lived—or at the very least superior to the one before it.

"I suppose you think that nobody can 'party' like you can, least of all an old fossil like me," I began.

Nicholas looked amused as he spun around in his chair. "I should take you to a party at my bro Flogger's house sometime."

"Not so fast. I might be able to teach your crowd a thing or two."

"Yeah, I'm sure you could," he said with a laugh.

"For instance, the best parties are held and attended by people who *want* to party."

"That would be my crew, bigtime."

"No, your 'crew' parties because it *needs* to."

Nicholas' expression changed. "What do you mean by that?"

I could sense Nicholas' young co-workers nearby suddenly growing attentive. I sat down on the edge of a worktable and continued. "Every generation has to party until it discovers its purpose and *earns* its fame. That's how they fill the void. Eventually something will happen to energize your generation, and then partying will be a *complementary* thing instead of the *main* thing."

The co-workers eagerly looked to Nicholas for a response. "Times have changed. We don't need something to happen *to us*. We make our own things happen." Like chimps, the group nodded their heads in satisfied agreement.

"Well, you may not understand this, but any purpose you give yourself will be unsatisfactory. Real purpose must discover *you*. There are two paths to fame—achievement and martyrdom. Your generation is still stuck with the latter."

H: *Formal Galas*

The same principle applies at work. The work is the main thing, and parties afterward are an outgrowth of success and achievements. It is a sad state of affairs indeed when you enter a firm where smoking and drinking are the main activities, and client projects are an afterthought. Such a company is not long for this world.

At my company we worked hard, and *then* we played hard. Sometimes management took the lead, and at other times the arrangements were made by the staff. I have mingled with elite guests while hosting lavish holiday galas where champagne sparkled in crystal glasses and ice-carved swans adorned the foyer, and I have excused myself from cheap get-togethers where Bud Lite bottles littered the kitchen table, and the only ice on display was the bag somebody picked up from the 7 Eleven. The latter is fine when you're just starting out: You'll find the liquor flows freely among both genders, and snaring the opposite sex requires little effort or imagination.

N: *Impromptu Parties*

Hub is too modest to admit it, but he's pretty good at cooking up casual gatherings. For most executives, the best office parties are spontaneous. Because they come together at the last minute, no one has a chance to invite along spouses, friends, and significant others to spoil the affair.

Here's a typical recipe for a memorable occasion.

> 5 hardboiled execs
> 5 lightly browned secretaries
> 1 half-dozen dimmed lights
> 1 pickled bartender
> 2 dozen harmless-looking blender drinks
> 3 bottles white wine
> 4 bags salty, empty-calorie chips
> 4 CDs fun music
> 8 small tables ideal for pairing off
> Hefty helping of bullshitting
> Generous pinch of flattery
> 1 fresh promotion
> 1 frozen clock

Blend execs and secretaries with small tables, then sprinkle with fun music and bullshitting. If boyfriend inadvertently arrives, slice and grate immediately. Sauté secretaries in wine sauce, add pinch, and roll out promotion. Mix rest of ingredients thoroughly, bake at high heat, and serve dish hot. Season to taste and don't worry about the time. (May use less dimmed lights if necessary.)

I don't know for sure, but I think this is the same recipe Hub used to win over Brittany.

H: *No Monopoly*

Not exactly. Nicholas' recipe is missing "1 stale wife." While I'm at it, let me point out that when it comes to hanky-panky, Nicholas' generation is hardly pure. In fact, they make mine look like monks.

N: *No Kidding*

Hub may be right—some of us were definitely paying attention during biology class. Here's the difference though: We don't pretend to be monks.

H: *Etiquette*

While you may feel comfortable with your "anything goes" sexuality, there are a significant number of rules that you ought to learn to follow if you are to feel comfortable during certain other activities, such as executive luncheons.

Ablebright's Etiquette Tips

1) A doggie bag for your leftover palate cleanser is a no-no. (You do have some left, don't you?)

2) Butter only one piece of bread, cut only one piece of meat, and eat only one bite at a time. (Since you shouldn't speak with your mouth full, this will make it easier to swallow whole whatever you're chewing before responding to a question.)

3) If you must excuse yourself to go to the restroom, leave your napkin on your chair. (Do not hand it to the waiter or toss it on the table. Do not take the napkin with you—unless you need to flush away the stubborn chunks of gristle that you have been discreetly spitting into the napkin throughout the meal.)

4) Do not caper about The Waldorf exchanging dessert samples with diners at neighboring tables. (You may, however, share samples with guests seated next to you by leaving tidbits in your napkin on your chair when you excuse yourself to use the restroom. This presumes, of course, that you have already disposed of your gristle.)

5) Do not butter vegetables—to do so is an insult to the chef. (*Not* eating *any* of the dry, tasteless crap is apparently less of an insult.)

6) Eat pickles with your fingers when they accompany sandwiches. Use a knife and fork when pickles are served with meat. (You'll need every sharp object you can get your hands on to fight off the rabid vegetarians that suddenly appear.)

7) Using bread to soak up the extra gravy on your plate is a compliment to the chef. (Chef Pierre is finally catching on!)

8) When garnishes are passed around on a relish tray they should never go directly into your mouth. (Touch them with your fingers first.)

9) Never pick up a chop and gnaw at it—even when it's wearing a panty, which is a paper sleeve around the bone. (Don't even get me started.)

10) When unsure of yourself, simply follow the lead of the host—
within reason. (I remember one clod from the Midwest who
was so nervous he mimicked *everything* I did. I took a bite of
salad, he took a bite of salad. I wiped my chin with my
napkin, he wiped his chin with his napkin, and so on.
Annoyed, I decided to sit perfectly still and say nothing. For
a half-hour neither of us moved or made a sound. It
reminded me of dinner dates with my first wife.)

N: *More Etiquette*
Hub neglected to mention that you should hold a chilled wineglass by the
stem as you sip from it. Likewise, hold a chilled bottle by the neck as you
drink.

H: *Cocktails For Every Occasion*
Over the years, I have ordered all of the following cocktails as
events dictated. They became way-markers in my life. Now, when
somebody orders one, or I see the name of one mentioned, I am
instantly taken back to the appropriate occasion. I hope that you,
too, will develop a similarly rich history.

Boomerang
Can't remember the precise occasion. I'm sure it will come back to
me in a minute or two.

Bosom
Never order anymore—reminds me too much of Mother Goose.

Brainstorm
To all those people who think I've never had one—you're wrong.

Bunny Hug
Where else—our conference in '74 at the Playboy Club.

Climax, Lovers' Delight
Hard to pinpoint—I've had so many of both.

Dizzy
The circumstances are a bit blurry, but I do remember I also had
a *Platinum Blonde* that night.

Elephant's Ear, Horse's Neck
The two drinks I ordered during the last blind date I ever went on. Tried to dull my mind with a **Zombie.** Can't recall much else until she showed up at my office the next day to return my watch. Then, I had an **Emergency.**

Fallen Angel
Doubt whether I'll ever get to have one of these again, since first I would have to *fall.*

Flu
Tasted best on warm, sunny Fridays at the club.

Fuzzy Navel
I may have had a few of these, but I was apparently too preoccupied to notice.

Garden Of Eden, Goddess Of Love, and Kiss From Heaven
Whenever I needed divine intervention.

Goat's Delight
Can't remember why I ordered one of these—must have been at a time when I would drink anything.

Honeymoon, Frankenstein
Don't ever order these together! Instead, try **Honeymoon** with **Symphony Of Moist Joy**—much better.

Hari Kari, Six Feet Under
For some reason having the first usually lead to getting the other.

Irresistible
I was alone at the racquet club and feeling a little sorry for myself, because I had just gotten beat on the court by a younger man. What I needed from the bartender was a **Gloom Lifter,** but he had something else in mind instead and slid a **Tennis Girl** down the bar at me. Looked and smelled just like a **Tempter.** I told the bartender to get something for the young lady and introduced myself. All she replied was, "**Shirley Temple.**" I should have left immediately, but before too long I had **Three Fourths**

and I wanted to finish it off. Just as things were heating up she let slip to the bartender, "I'd really like to drain a **Millionaire** dry." That hit me harder than **TNT** on a **Mule's Hind Leg**. I jumped out of there so fast I didn't even have time for one **Last Thought**.

Maiden's Prayer
My drink of choice when I took a new secretary out. Of course, she never had one. I would suggest a **Whip**, but she usually ended up with an **Eye Opener**.

Nude Eel
First served up one of these at my chalet in Vail. My relationship with Brittiny was just getting serious. She insisted on an **Oh, Henry!** and for the rest of the evening we had a pitcher of **Paradise**.

Royal Screw
Especially satisfying after I'd taken over another small company. I'd invite them over to celebrate, drink in all I could of an **Egghead,** and then I'd send them all away with a **Fare-Thee-Well**.

Sabbath Calm
My attractive and extremely busy neighbor set aside one for herself every week. She promised that not even an **Earthquake** or a **Hurricane** could supplant her routine. That, of course, was before I sauntered over one afternoon and introduced her to **Satan's Whiskers**.

Sex On The Beach
It was a dark and hazy night when I first gave this one a try. My date got all excited when her **Malibu Wave** arrived. Suddenly, there was a **Foghorn** next to me.

Twinkle Toes
I was at a conference in San Francisco. An associate of mine, a VP from marketing, had one of these when he started snuggling up to a transvestite. I ordered a **Which Way,** drank that, and then sat back to see how the whole thing would turn out with **Anna's Banana**.

Wedding Belle
Had one of these when I needed to come to my senses quickly.

N: *Too Complicated*
Those are all *drink* names? Just give me a beer and be done with it.

While we're on the subject of drinking, did you know that the Babylonian gods made *two* judgments when they heard a case? First, they heard the case sober and made a decision; then, they got drunk, heard the case again, and made a second decision.

H: *More Fun, But Not Too Smart*
That kind of setup would give jury duty a whole new image. Just one question. What did they do when the two decisions contradicted each other?

N: *Just Guessing*
That must be where drugs came in.

H: *"Snow"*
I figured you'd mention drugs sooner or later. It has become fashionable among the "chic" generation of professionals to disdain the traditional libations I listed previously in favor of trendy designer drugs such as cocaine. If you are one of these young "cokeheads," I urge you to pick yourself up by your bootstraps, give up drugs, and start drinking instead. The delusional effect of drugs might actually lead you to believe you can start a company that will make millions on the Internet. The worst that can happen when you're drinking is you make a few promises that are a bit too optimistic. More overtime hours by your staff will easily cover it.

If we don't do something about drugs soon, society is destined to go to hell in a handbasket.

N: *We Didn't Invent It*
Drugs have been around a long time. Older people act like the young are

the first and only ones to ever experiment with drugs. I seem to recall some guy named Edgar Allen Poe getting awfully strung out way back in 1850-something.

H: *You Sure Act Like You Invented It*

It always amuses me that drug addicts refer to their usage as "experimenting," as though giving the proceedings a scientific tone will somehow legitimize it. Are we to imagine a lab and test tubes where the conscientious young "experimenter" discovers to his complete surprise that if he snorts cocaine up his nose or shoots heroin into his arm, he will begin to feel euphoric and hallucinate? And, all the while our little white-coated "scientist" meticulously records his reactions and vital signs for future review in the next issue of *Scientific American*.

Of course, what's the value of an experiment without corraboration? "Oh, no, officer, this isn't a party—they're just here to verify my initial hypothesis."

H: *The Retirement Party*

Drugs or no drugs, I had dreaded my retirement party, and rightly so. Mother Goose and Gadabout Parrot ushered me around like I was some kind of invalid, babbling apologies on my behalf.

"Oh, Hub won't be needing that anymore, Diane. And be sure to tell Harry that he's on his own now!" they cackled.

All of my enemies—Snarler Pit Bull, Backstabber Snake, and Ms. Lawsuit Vulture—pretended to like me for half an hour. They shook my hand and made stupid statements like, "Well, we didn't always see eye-to-eye, but we got the job done, didn't we!"

The Too Quiet Termites, who never attended any company function, showed up together for five minutes, squinted at me, awkwardly mumbled something, then faded back into their shadowy caverns.

Exaggerator Rooster excitedly told Complainer Crow, "If I play my cards right, I'll be able to retire by 40!" Crow crossed her arms and grumbled, "I'll be 80 before I get out of this hole."

Easily Offended Horse marched out early because I didn't hug her when she came through the reception line. Double-Jobber

Ant, whose beeper went off, trotted right behind her.

Ms. Envy Hyena stared at me jealously throughout, secretly wishing *she* were the one retiring. Ladder Climber Monkey slipped out of the party for a few minutes to take measurements of my office.

Hanger-On Bat shuffled over, patted me on the back, and chuckled something about outlasting me. Early Retiree Panda told me to look him up when I was in Palm Springs.

Clown Otter, on behalf of all the employees, presented me with a gag gift. One last time Flirt Peacock batted her eyelashes at me hopefully. Bubbly Chipmunk told me cheerfully how much her grandparents were enjoying their retirement, and that I should stop by if I ever got to Arkansas, because they'd love to have me stay a few days.

Oblivious Olive asked me if I knew who was retiring. Then, seeing my puzzled expression, said apologetically, "Oh, I'm sorry, you must be new here."

Do-It-All Octopus scurried past me a hundred times carrying cheese plates and punch cups, and later a bundle of paper towels to show Kindergartner Fawn how to clean up a spill.

They had set up big-screen televisions and a video feed to all of the company's plants and warehouses, so the rank-and-file could participate in the festivities. I gave a nice speech, but there was no need to get sentimental. It's not like I was leaving completely. I still have my keys to the building and the opportunity to reserve the corporate jet for the next five years. Then, of course, there is the ongoing consultant work I'm getting paid for.

N: *My Turn Someday Too*

Not to take the spotlight away from Hub, but I can hardly wait for my own retirement. I've got big plans for that $4.67 Social Security check.

H: Don't spend it all in one place! Hey, all kidding aside, the government's lockbox will ensure that you don't lose a penny.

N: Grrrr. . . .

18

GOLF

H: *The Official Sport Of Business*

Nowhere else will you find idyllic leisure so tantalizingly close at hand. Greens are manicured to tolerances within one-sixteenth of an inch. Butterflies dance in the breezes among colorful flowers and the sun warms the back of your neck as you stroll between carpeted fairways, the scent of clover in your nostrils. On the next tee over, beyond the pines, you hear the sweet impact of the club head and the ball—then the desperate curses of the player following its wayward flight.

Golf is the traditional sport of executives in many parts of the world. As I often instructed Nicholas, it is on the green Elysian links where the relationships are forged that lead to the real business getting done. I expressly warned him that the celebrated dot-com companies failed because their founders spent their lunches standing in a circle playing saki-hack, or whatever it's called, instead of being out on the golf course.

"Why do we always have to meet everyone at the golf course?" Nicholas asked me.

"Because that's just the way it's always been." The kid had a knack for asking some of the strangest questions.

N: *Chairman Of The Board*
And, Hub had a knack for giving some of the strangest answers.

"Why don't we ever play golf with the execs from Yodaco?" I asked.

"Yodaco? Well, ah, their execs don't play a lot of golf. It's against their religion—sort of like the Amish."

"Oh."

Executive-types get in some mega-deep ruts. Golf is almost like a religion to them (sort of like the Amish). To keep the creative juices flowing, you've got to taste new things on a regular basis. But every week it was off to the golf course with Hub and a client or some VIP for yet another round. Now, I don't mind golfing, but just once I would have liked to hit the street somewhere for some serious boarding.

"C'mon, Hubster, I'll show you how to do a backside kickturn."

I'll bet most clients would enjoy a little variety.

H: *Pay Your Dues*
I'd have turned and kicked somebody's backside all right.

Now, where was I? Do not try to *close* any deals while on the course. Trying to do so will only irritate the players, who are intent on making par. Your objective is merely to set the stage with introductory remarks such as, "We've got some great prices on [fill in the blank] at this time of year." The place to close the deal is at a cozy table in the clubhouse after a satisfying round. And, the only way the round is going to be satisfying is if they beat you and enjoy themselves in the process.

As the junior member of the foursome you are expected to lose regularly. This is not as tough to swallow for your generation as it was for mine. Like most people his age, Nicholas had more opportunities to golf than I ever did growing up. Consequently, he was a better player at age 25 than I was, but I had far more competitive fire. When I told Nicholas he was expected to lose, he merely shrugged his shoulders and said, "Whatever." I, on the other hand, would grit my teeth and work myself up into such a lather that by the time we reached the back nine I couldn't see to hit the ball straight, which was just as well since that guaranteed my defeat.

N: *Honorable Excuses*

Those old guys are just insane about beating each other. They bet on practically every hole and threaten each other with their nine irons. I really didn't care who won, but I still had to maintain my dignity. I built up a repertoire of excuses for some of the bad shots I had to take.

- "My wrist just isn't the same since I started professional arm wrestling."

- "My darn back is acting up again. Must be that new position she had me try."

- "I test clubs for the PGA, and they just sent me a new set. It's going to take me a while to get used to them."

- "I don't understand it. I shot a 68 out here two days ago."

- "It's my first time on an American course in three years. The courses overseas are so different."

- "I was expecting the sun to be shining in my good eye, so I overcompensated."

H: *Hedge Your Bets*

Further protect yourself by "half-shaving" your score. Everybody knocks three to four shots off their score. Some of the more senior execs even "double-shave" to gain a true advantage, taking six to eight off their scores. You, however, should never shave more than one or two shots if you're truly committed to losing.

N: *When Losing Is A Challenge*

Some of the clients in our foursomes played so poorly they yelled, "Fore!" after *every* shot simply out of habit. You could swing broom handles and still beat them. I remember partnering with Hub once when one of the players in our foursome swung his clubs like a drunken Abe Lincoln chopping wood. More than once the old goat stood over the ball in his knickers, wiggled his rump, took a swing, and nubbed his ball about three feet off the tee. He was an important client, so we kept our mouths stuffed with extra golf balls to avoid laughing.

Near the middle of the round, this duffer claimed his game was "coming back" to him. He stood proudly on the par-three eleventh tee watching his ball land after swinging wildly and crowed, "Bingo! On the green in one."

I leaned over to Hub and whispered, "Who's gonna tell him he's on the *ninth* green?"

On the next tee he hooked his ball toward the woods. Hub cringed. Miraculously, the ball hit a large oak tree and ricocheted back out into the middle of the fairway. The old sagger had no idea which direction his tee shot had gone.

"You guys see it?"

"It's right there in the middle of the fairway," I said with a sigh.

"Once I get on a roll—look out!" He then did a little jig that was a cross between the "Macarena" and the "Chicken Dance."

That was the only time he hit safely all day. In the end, there was nothing we could do but take the attention off him when it was our turn by whiffing at the ball or whacking it into the woods at a 45-degree angle. (Hub and I laughed about it for weeks afterward in the office, aping the client's goofy swings whenever we passed in the hallway.)

The worst thing about this client was he insisted on playing *another* round in a sorry attempt to redeem himself. "Aw, c'mon, Hub—let's go again. I'm warmed up now."

H: *Protocol*

You know how to address the ball—but how do you address the senior executives in your foursome? Young professionals naturally tend to be lax, so it behooves you to pay special attention here. You might think that since you're away from the office, formalities have ceased. You'd be dead wrong. Remember, I said the golf course is where some of the most important groundwork is laid for major business deals. Think of the sun-dappled fairways as your second office. In fact, when I take along one of my junior partners, the others in the group think he's merely keeping score—and he is—but you can be assured he's also taking *notes*.

With this in mind, consider carefully these guidelines for what to call senior execs.

- **"Sir"**
  Acceptable, but use sparingly. Patronizing if overused.

- **"Mr. Smith"**
  The last name preceded by "Mr." is always safe.

- **"Jim"**
  Don't you dare use his first name. The only exceptions would be after a hole-in-one or perhaps after he taps in on the final hole for a new personal best score. A gentle "Nice shot, Jim" or "Nice round, Jim" would be appropriate in these contexts in light of the good feelings generated by the event.

- **"Chief"**
  Too flippant for newcomers.

- **"Your Excellency"**
  A bit overdone.

- **Just nod your head.**
  Only afterward in the locker room or club.

N: *Protocol, Part Two*

I called a vice president "dude" one time when I was tired and forgot where I was. Fortunately, the VP didn't hear it—he still had water in his ears from a little episode involving a pond earlier in the round.

While we're on the subject of protocol, you should hear the way Hub and his cronies refer to women on the golf course. It's not like they're joking around—they don't even realize what they're saying! They toss these terms around so casually and naturally that they don't even care if the women hear them.

"Hey, babe, nice shot! . . . I know where she can get lucky again."

"That hot number can grip my putter any time."

"Hey, kitten! Join us for a drink afterwards?"

"Ain't she a looker? Tell her I'd like to play a round."

"Look at the set of blossoms on that tomato!"

"What a doll! But she needs to practice her stroke. Let her know I'm available for private lessons."

"Oh, let's not get in the way of Dinah." (As in Dinah Shore—a woman who takes golfing seriously.)

"What does that dame think she's doing with that driver?"

"That broad couldn't hit the green if she tossed it up there."

"Have a look-see at that dish, will you? That clump of hair sticking up over her visor makes her look like Big Bird."

"Did you see that bim? I've seen better swings at a playground."

"We'd get done a lot faster if these skirts would get off the course. I was going to join Augusta until I found out they let women play as guests."

Hub and his partners also considered whistling to be acceptable. I'll bet they lost business with those comments and didn't even realize it.

H: *Golf Etiquette*

The ladies always enjoyed a little attention, but I was all business when I stepped on the tee. Golf has a long history and is taken very seriously by the men who play it. There are rules of conduct that govern play for the respect and safety of others. Though "rules" seem to carry less weight among your more independently minded peers, you should be aware that if you break one of these rules at certain prestigious courses you might never be permitted back again.

1) **Do not carry your cell phone with you on the course.**
   If you want to see blood in the eyes of otherwise civilized men, watch their reaction when somebody's phone rings on the tee. It had better be your doctor calling, because you're going to need him.

2) **Beware as you approach the tee in the Sunshine State.**
   That gator coming up behind you means business. Remain calm, and let him play through.

3) **It is a breach of etiquette to pound your tee into the dirt with your club after a disappointing shot.**
   You may, however, *stomp* it into the ground with your shoe.

4) **Take mulligans in moderation.**
   Especially when you're playing two balls.

5) **Do not talk or make any noises while players are hitting the ball.**
   There is one exception, if you are clever enough to pull it off. In my younger days I played with a senior exec who hated to

lose. Problem was, his putting was erratic. On the final hole, with the match on the line, I coughed intentionally an instant after he stroked his putt. The ball had been safely away, but I wanted to give him an out in case he missed—which he did. I apologized profusely and insisted he try the putt again. Not surprisingly, he accepted. With the benefit of having read the line on the first attempt, he hitched up his trousers, puffed on his cigar, and holed the second putt, which satisfied him immensely.

6) Do not touch somebody else's ball.
Again, there is a reasonable exception, provided you are not discovered. If you find a senior exec's ball in a miserable lie, you may tap it slightly with your foot wedge to a more congenial location before he arrives to play it.

7) When you finally leave a sand trap there should be no evidence that you were ever there.
This rule applies more appropriately to senior players, and it has nothing to do with footprints. It means no evidence *on the scorecard.*

8) On the green, mark your ball with something smaller than a silver dollar.
And here you'd thought you had finally found a use for all of those compact discs you keep getting from America Offline.

9) Use discretion with "gimmes."
The general rule is one foot away from the hole for each decade of management experience. Since you have less than ten years in, expect to putt everything out.

10) Always keep track of where you parked the golf cart.
The others in your foursome will ridicule you unmercifully if you lose it. (And do not ride off in somebody else's cart, no matter how desperate you are to save face.)

H: *The Passionate Player*
Successful executives are strong-willed and passionate about what they do. Being high-spirited is not a weakness, and you'd

better not react to it as such. One of your foursome may occasionally fling a club in your direction. Simply get out of the way. But what if he throws his bag into the pond? Choose one of the following answers to see how prepared you are.

A. Immediately wade in after his clubs, fish them out, dry them as best you can, and return them.

B. Find an excuse to throw one of your own clubs into the pond, go in after it, then off-handedly retrieve his set too since you're already there anyway.

C. Watch the entire incident, as Nicholas did, with an air of amused, ironic detachment.

D. Hide fearfully behind a tree until the whole episode is over.

If you answered "A," you are bordering on being labeled a Suck-up Sturgeon and will never be anything but an assistant manager. Answering "B" confirms you are well on your way to occupying an executive suite. If you answered "C," you'd probably rather be disc golfing. Finally, if you responded "D," you had better not be around if a proud executive ever misses a two-foot putt with money on the line.

N: *Meltdown*

Actually, Hub did miss a two-foot putt once, causing him to lose to me by one stroke. He got all spazzed out about it because based on his "level of service" he supposedly qualified for a "gimme." He railed on me for not giving it to him. Hey, in my mind, you don't get nothin' for free. Life is hard, and then you die. He was so ticked off that he fired his favorite four-leaf clover silver ball marker into a bunker. I could tell he immediately regretted it. He'd told me a million times that marker had been given to him by his dad, who had died a few years ago.

H: *Speed Golfers*

Not content with ruining ski hills with their goatees and snowboards, your generation's extremists have now taken aim at quiet, venerable golf courses with an absurdity known as "speed golf" or "aerobic golf." The record is something like thirty-eight minutes to complete one round.

Piles of divots in his wake, one of these maniacs will literally come running up behind you, panting and dragging four or five clubs, and screaming something about having to play through. He'll race up to his ball, swing away at it, then chase after it, sometimes even hitting it again before it lands. The effect on the rest of us is unnerving to say the least.

I confess I had a strategy to frustrate these sideshow freaks, but I was never in the right place at the right time. At the fringe of each green they may momentarily drop their clubs while rushing to putt. I intended to snatch the clubs and hide them among my own. Due to the scrambled state of his brain (for which the entire experience has been a blur), the speed demon will have no idea where he last put the clubs or, for that matter, how long he has been playing without them. It would have been fun to see how fast he finished the rest of the course using only his putter.

N: *Speed Golfers, Part Two*
Personally, I think speed golfing is a rush (literally). I've seen tightwads spend more time looking for a lost ball than I spend playing nine holes.

H: *The Company Golf Outing*
I have always felt that company golf outings border on sacrilege. Everybody from silly receptionists to uncoordinated computer geeks are invited along for a day of "fun and frolic." Consecrated tees, hallowed fairways, and sacred greens are subjected to all manner of disrespect and tomfoolery. Imagine some clod from maintenance in a tank top and cowboy boots walking across your beautiful greens, or two silly secretaries in high heels giggling as they swing rented putters at the ball on the first tee.

Then you've got Snarler Pit Bull cussing up a storm after every shot he butchers, Complainer Crow whining about the weather, and Exaggerator Rooster crowing about the one shot he hit solidly all day. Gadabout Parrot circles the course in her festooned golf cart handing out cheap prizes, Double-Jobber Ant disappears into the woods to look for his ball and returns two hours later with a part from one of his customer's water heaters in his golf bag, and Suck-Up Sturgeon keeps telling you at every step that he's never seen a better shot than the one you just nailed. Sundialer Sloth and Hanger-On Bat do nothing but hold up play. Clown Otter nearly kills you with his golf cart just before it tips over. Hypochondriac Guinea Pig is injured by an errant golf ball, Pinball Salmon takes a 23 on one hole before you finally grab his ball out of the sand trap and fling it onto the green, and Handwringer Chihuahua spends the day worrying about the divots that nobody's replacing. Finally, there's Oblivious Olive, taking aim at the green while players are still putting, and picking up and pocketing balls lying in the fairway that she thought were lost. Don't let her drive the cart—she'll take a wrong turn on the path and wind up on the highway or an airport runway.

In the early days of my career, I had no choice but to put up with this travesty or schedule my sick days so as to avoid the outing altogether. After having countless scenes of wild swings, hooks, slices, nubs, and various other antics burned into my mind's eye, I would play horribly for days afterward until the images were finally purged from my system.

Once I rose to the rank of CEO, I no longer endorsed such outings and consequently they were removed from my company's social calendar.

H: *Final Word*

Some wag once wrote, "Golf is a good walk ruined." That's why I always rent a cart.

19

CORPORATE MERGERS

H: *Just Settle Down*

There is *no* need for this chapter, because there is *no* planned merger! It's all just a rumor, and there's *no* substance to any of it.

And besides, even if it were to happen, the regular employees would *not* be affected. The only changes would be minor administrative ones. *No* plant or office closings are planned. It would be pretty much business as usual.

The only thing that might change would be the health insurance carrier. And, a few mid-level managers might have to move to North Carolina. Other than that, you would hardly notice the difference.

There's a remote chance, hardly worth mentioning, that one or two tiny departments, like personnel, could be consolidated. A handful of people affected at most. Of course, we'd also have to switch our network and operating systems over to NT so everything is compatible, but that only makes sense.

One other thing we had planned to do regardless, due to disappointing performance, was phase out the e-commerce division. This would speed that up a bit, but like I said, it was on the chopping block anyway.

Bottom line: We're stronger and healthier than ever. Pay no attention to any merger talk.

N: *Needed Reassurance*

Everyone is so glad to finally know where things stand.

20

FEMALE EXECUTIVES

H: *The Stakes Are High*

You may have noticed the male-oriented approach to this book and the general absence of advice for prospective lady professionals and executives. This has not been by accident.

We have Mary Kay and Sara Lee to thank for instilling women with the idea that they could lead billion-dollar companies. If it had stopped with makeup companies and the like, we would have had little to quarrel with. After all, few men desire to head cosmetics firms or pie companies. Unfortunately, women built confidence in these fields, and then were encouraged to step out further, into areas traditionally dominated by men. Believe me when I tell you their ultimate goal is to *outnumber* us and earn *more* than us. Men and women have been in competition for ages, and we would be kidding ourselves to think the battle has ended.

Nowadays, there are even girls trying to play high school football, for Pete's sake. I'll tell you, if they had tried that in my heyday, they would've been knocked flat before they ever got out of the huddle.

N: *Diversity*

Hub's idea of diversity at work is Coke and Sprite together in the same vending machine.

"The world can't handle diversity. It leads to conflict every time," he told me once, ramming his fists together.

H: *"Bully Broads" Training*

I'm not against anybody trying to make a living. I hired all kinds in my time. Usually, there were few problems as long as everyone learned their place. I had no trouble with lady managers and executives when these gals acted as much like men as possible. Fortunately, for the past few decades this was the norm. Female traits were viewed as a weakness in the boardroom and women adapted accordingly by wearing pantsuits and ties, favoring short haircuts, and conducting themselves in a hardened, assertive manner. The result was a watered down copy of the best in the typical male executive, one that real men could relate to and easily deal with.

Times are changing, however. There is a dangerous movement afoot to convince America that a more female-centered leadership style is preferable to the tried-and-true approach that has guided this country's industry for over a century. As a result, otherwise tolerable lady managers are coaxed into spending several days at retreats designed to soften their approach and take the man (that is, the bully) out of them.

Sometimes known as "Ice Queen" Training, these sessions teach high-level women to get rid of the tough, aggressive, and cutthroat style that propelled their climb. Instead the sessions brainwash lady executives into getting back in touch with their sensitive, emotional, and intuitive sides.

N: *Reality Bites*

"So, Janelle, do you think you'll ever make VP?" I asked as we sat down in the lunchroom.

"Oh, yes, definitely."

"Here?"

She nearly choked on her bottled water. "I'll let you answer that one yourself."

"Have you been looking anywhere?"

"No, but I'm sure something will pop up. Companies are always looking to cut costs, and one way to do that is by hiring women in management. They don't have to pay us as much."

H: *Repercussions Of Female Leadership Style*

Salaries aside, ladies in management positions are, of course, a bad fit and they know it, which is why they seek to change the rules. They realize they cannot match our strengths, so they have now begun to discredit us and promote their own inborn feminine qualities as preferable in the business arena. Imagine the repercussions of this new "sensitive-emotional-intuitive" managerial approach if it ever takes over.

For starters, golf outings would become excursions through hell. Women are, of course, miserable golfers, which is bad enough when they're playing on their own. If they were to take over more chairmanships with their new leadership style, we might have to begin playing in mixed foursomes. Criminy! Can you imagine having a lady in your foursome and, because she is your boss or a potential client, having to *lose* to her? Oh, that's right, I forgot. The new, softened ladies wouldn't view winning and losing in the same way we men do. Hence . . .

> **Lady CEO (in large hat and stockings):** "Gretchen, what was your score on that hole?"
>
> **Lady client (taking out her compact):** "Oh, Morgan, I don't remember! For Goodness' sake, that cute greens keeper distracted me. Just put me down for a 2."
>
> **Lady CEO:** "Hub, what did you have?"
>
> **Me:** "I told you—a 6!"
>
> **Lady CEO:** "Hub, you need to see someone about that temper of yours. Oh, well, it doesn't matter anyway—I lost the scorecard."

Next, we'd have to change the destinations where we take clients and hold some of our meetings. The new sensitive lady executive would never stand for an enthusiastic evening at the gentlemen's club. Better start making reservations at the local tearoom.

Lady client (extending saucer and doily): "Here, Hub, try the Hibiscus Passion Tea. This will get your blood flowing."
Me (waking up): "Better start me with a half cup—I don't know if my heart can take all that passion."

Forget about implementing urgent austerity measures such as downsizing and offshore outsourcing. In the highly unlikely event that an emotional lady CEO would have the heart to give anyone the axe, surely it would only be after months of counseling.

Lady VP of personnel (with worried brow): "I'm so sorry, Erica, but the company faces bankruptcy if we don't let a few people go. We'll understand if you don't want to leave right away. Could you possibly transition out of your office in six months?"
Employee: "But Ms. Higgins, by then I may have bought a new house, and my boyfriend and I will probably be pregnant."
Lady VP of personnel (moving forward for a hug): "Oh, Erica! I'm so glad you said something. We'll move Ablebright out instead. Come see me tomorrow about a raise. And, would it help if we had childcare on-site?"

Hiring new employees would be another fiasco.

Prospective employee: "You're not going to hold that little embezzling thing against me, are you?"
Lady personnel manager (tenderly laying a hand on the individual's arm): "No . . . of course not. We don't beat people up over the past here. Besides, I just have this feeling—call it women's intuition—that you're the right accountant for us."

You can bet the decision-making process would be hamstrung by the consensus-building trait of this new breed of leaders.

Lady CEO (hopefully): "So, we all agree then—we'll expand to Europe early next year."
Male board member: "Hey, I thought we were gonna consider China."

Lady CEO: "China? Okay, we can work with that."

Other male board member: "China sucks. Europe makes far more sense."

Lady CEO: "I can see the only way to solve this is to compromise. Not everyone has to win or lose. Therefore, we'll meet each other half way and open our new office in Pakistan."

The only silver lining would be the improved treatment that attractive secretaries would receive from chastened and newly sensitive lady supervisors. The prettiest secretaries currently face undeserved hardship as they endure the spitefulness of the older, flat-chested, and jealous lady executives.

Old . . .

Plain-faced lady exec: "Stop flashing your eyelids, Tiffany—that doesn't work with me. If you want to get ahead, you're going to have to type more than twenty-five words per minute."

Tiffany (wiping her cheeks): "Yes, Ms. Bentley."

Lady exec: "And stop that blubbering—that doesn't work with me, either."

New . . .

Plain-faced lady exec: "You know, Tiff, I've been terribly hard on you in the past."

Tiffany (cautiously): "You have?"

Lady exec (humbly): "Yes, I have. The truth is, I'm a bird-faced frump and you're an enchanting angel. It's time I began to value you for your strengths."

Tiffany (comfortingly): "Oh, Ms. Bentley, you are *not* a frump. I think you're wonderful."

Lady exec (stiffening): "Who cares what you think, you airheaded twit."

Tiffany gasps.

Lady exec (catching herself): "Oh, dear me! Another flashback. Be patient with me, Tiffany—I can't be expected to change completely overnight."

N: *Pent-Up Demand*

Hub believes there is yet another reason to oppose the softening of women managers, but he's too bashful to come right out and say it.

It is well known that an aggressive, hardened, high-powered male who spends his day fighting to finally get over the hump builds up physical tension that quickly reaches a climax. Racquetball and weightlifting provide some release, but nothing pops the cork like you know what.

Do you think the situation is any less dire for a young female manager struggling to be assertive and intimidating in a high-pressure world? She arrives home with perhaps twice the tension built up from straddling the pressures we all face—plus the mounting burden of pretending to be something she's not.

"Believe me when I say those gals are aching for a little pleasure by the time they spread themselves in exhaustion on the couch at the end of a long day," Hub confided.

A syndicated female newspaper columnist once laid bare this very issue. The main point of the column was this analogy: "All those aggressive female primates, after a busy day of dominating their jungle, were primed for sex, not for the withholding of it."

If women managers are allowed to cultivate a more relaxed leadership style, executives following in Hub's footsteps will have nobody left but their secretaries to turn to for relief.

21

MENTORS

H: *Principles In Action*

I am confident you will find the pointers, insights, and instructions I have provided throughout the first twenty chapters to be worth their weight in gold as you kick off your career. Nevertheless, there's nothing like seeing the principles I have described in action. While I can't take you personally into the arena of executive achievement, I can at least provide the accounts of real-life executives and their inspiring exploits, summarized here for you from my personal contacts.

The inspiration for this chapter comes from a dear friend in the business world who in many ways mentored *me*. He took every opportunity to expose ill-gotten gain, to uncover deceitfulness, and to denounce evil of every sort in the workplace. He trumpeted such righteousness and purity, and cultivated an image so beyond reproach—that he could readily get away with just about anything.

"Wanna be a hero?" he asked me once. "After they've badgered you for walking off with $500 million, tell them your gut told you to give $10 million back. They'll worship ya."

Many of the following anecdotes have received coverage in newspapers and magazines. Although ordinarily I wouldn't hesitate to give proper credit to these exemplary men, I have chosen not to provide their names, lest these individuals be overwhelmed with disciples. These "paper mentors" will have to suffice until you find your own flesh-and-blood versions to guide you along.

H: *Supply And Demand*

I'll start with a heart-warming example that shows how well our free-enterprise system still works. One of those congressional reports that comes out now and then cited several internal memos from major oil companies that described a general strategy of tweaking supplies to influence prices. One memo listed time-honored strategies such as reducing production, shipping supplies to Canada, filling the limited capacity of pipelines with products other than gasoline, and providing incentives to other producers not to provide extra gasoline.

The report asserted that ". . . major refiners reduced gasoline production even in the face of unusually high demand . . . contributing significantly to the price spike." In the spring of 2000, when prices soared past $2 a gallon in some areas, the report claimed that at least one company held back some of its cleaner burning gasoline ". . . so as not to depress prices."

It's easy to admire the brilliance of this strategy. Nonetheless, the key in carrying it off lies in having the guts to follow through. Do not be intimidated by hypocritical politicians and consumers who have had plenty of opportunity to pursue alternative products, then later holler that they're being held hostage by a market of their own choosing.

H: *Cover Your Tracks*

Alternatives, however, are not always available. If, like many companies, you have no practical choice but to flush PCBs from your plant into the river, make sure there is another company *upstream* doing the same. That way, when the EPA comes snooping around, you can deny all wrongdoing, and the Feds will have no way to prove the compounds along your bend in the river aren't from that other company.

H: *Greatness Runs In The Family*

These legends raised the bar in so many ways it's tough to measure their true impact. For starters, in 1997 "Jr." inspired many of us by becoming the first U.S. businessman to take delivery on his very own Gulfstream G-V, a $38-million corporate jet. A short while later, "Sr." published his memoir, in which he took due credit for every pivotal business decision and good fortune the company enjoyed.

Sr.'s book is highly recommended for those of you looking for an example of how one man could single-handedly guide a company through challenge after challenge, saving it time and again from the sad fate that would have awaited it under a lesser man's rein. Though the book has its shortcomings, it is anything but the ". . . rambling, self-aggrandizing anecdotes of a conceited, pompous executive . . ." as one spiteful reviewer described it.

N: *Shoe Salesmen Have More Fun*

Just can't resist jumping in. I recently heard where the CEO of a major shoe company resigned after only three-and-a-half years at the helm. Supposedly, it was the company's lackluster bottom line that led to the CEO's flameout. They say his resignation had nothing to do with the lawsuit filed by his former assistant, which alleged the CEO had mistresses entertain him at the corporate apartment, on business excursions, and in the back of company limousines. Hub, I didn't know selling shoes could be so entertaining!

H: *Stand Tall*

I guess things have picked up since I sold my last pair of pumps. Don't worry about him though—he'll be back. "The path of success is paved with the stones of failure." Everybody trumpets sayings like that until a CEO is part of one of the failures. Then, they want to tar and feather him. Never mind the lazy workers beneath him who didn't get the job done. Pin it all on the CEO. Balderdash!

Stand up for your rights like the proud executives who have insisted on their multi-million dollar severance packages and bonuses despite their companies declaring bankruptcy. Even the fired coach of a last place team is paid out handsomely. Why should executives be treated any differently?

H: *Revenge Is Sweet*

One company president I know (let's call him "Red") was determined to build his new corporate headquarters on the waterfront. In the process of buying the large lakeside property he needed for the facilities, Red bucked horns with one particularly stubborn landowner. Several buildings were being constructed on the waterfront side of the road and the landowner's house stood on the landward side. But hold on, the landowner also owned a parcel on the waterfront side, giving him access to the lake.

The landowner knew Red needed his waterfront parcel and held out for a high price. Red finally agreed to the landowner's demands, but he didn't like being taken. The little landowner relished his victory over the sophisticated executive and his high-powered real estate team. True, he no longer had direct access to the lake and beach, but he still had his million-dollar view, and that was what really mattered.

Or, did he still have that view? Ol' Red had an ace up his sleeve—or in this case, a berm. Red's designers favored a heavily landscaped campus, with an especially tall berm directly across from the small landowner's bay window. Since there conveniently had been nothing in the property transfer deed about an easement to protect the landowner's view, there was nothing the landowner could do but watch his prized vista disappear with each shovel full of dirt.

N: *Can't Catch A Break*

That would be such a pleasant bedtime story for Hub's grandson. Here's another one.

Even though two auction houses together already controlled more than 90 percent of the world's art auctions, the former chairman of one of the houses was sentenced to prison and fined millions for his part in a price-fixing scheme that overcharged sellers by nearly $44 million.

"No one is above the law," the federal judge said.

The elderly chairman first tried influencing the judge against a harsh sentence by claiming prison time would worsen his fragile health. This is usually a successful strategy, but our friend couldn't catch a break. He cited heart disease, diabetes, hypertension and renal failure. The judge was like a stone wall. (Maybe the additional mention of heat rash or foot corns would have tipped the scales of justice in the chairman's favor.)

Next he played the "reputation" card. His lawyers pointed out that their client's ". . . once stellar reputation, which took him decades of incredibly hard work and humanity to build, has been shattered, literally overnight. The humiliation he has endured is simply indescribable."

Amazingly, the judge was again unmoved. He agreed that the former chairman's charitable contributions were substantial, but added that they were not unusual for a man worth more than $640 million.

H: *A Happy Ending*
Nicholas has a habit of only telling part of the story. And what's a story for my grandson without a lesson and a happy ending? The elderly chairman had a partner in the deal who left himself an out. A resident of merry old England, the head of the other auction house cannot be extradited to the United States on antitrust charges.

Here's another fairy tale ending for you. The Securities and Exchange Commission, no doubt with a dose of grudging admiration, identified one sharp executive who was able to receive a tax benefit by funding a building in his name at his college alma mater with donations of overvalued company stock.

H: *Only The Poor Pay Interest*
To cushion the cost of the down payment on his new house, a banking CEO friend of mine got himself an interest-free, $1-million loan from his firm. The far-sighted company pointed out that loans to its top honchos were part of its relocation package for executives who sucked it up and moved at the bank's request. The CEO's $6.8 million in compensation and stock-option grant valued at $34.5 million might have scared off lesser firms from offering that kind of loan, but this company stuck to its guns.

N: *Knowing When To Stop*
Rumor has it the same CEO turned down a complimentary toaster when

he opened a new savings account at his bank—no sense in creating the wrong appearance.

H: *Loose And Irresponsible*

You can learn from bad apples, too. Now and then, an eccentric company founder will see a bright light, feel a warm tingling in his heart, and get an irresponsible notion to share his profits equally with his workers. He'll set aside what should have been his $5-million bonus, and carve it up like a crazed psychopath, doling it out to everyone who ever pushed a broom at his company. Not only is this bad for his personal financial health, it's bad for the economy, too, since little—if any—of this distribution will be reinvested. Nor can companies expect higher productivity from workers who are now dreaming about that new boat they bought or their upcoming junket to Las Vegas.

N: *More Than Talk*

One company president recently earned headlines by having two of his assistants clip $25 gift certificates to all of the vehicles parked at "Share-a-Ride" lots along the metro freeways. He explained that he was tired of just talking about environmental stewardship and decided to reward those who were actually doing something positive. The vehicle owners thought it was way cool, of course, and he got a lot of good publicity for his cause.

H: *Wackos*

Can you imagine the repercussions if this kind of thing catches on? Tree-huggers will be lining up on the sidewalks outside our companies with their hands out, waiting for us to reward every silly thing they do. "Hey, Ablebright, I planted a tree—where's my $25?"

H: *Don't Lose Sight*

Don't ever forget: You are a businessman, not a savior. Avoid embroiling yourself in the problems of your local community, or you will lose sight of your core mission, which is to profitably produce your product or service.

One such foolish company saddled itself with cleaning up and revitalizing several blocks of a rundown urban area instead of building its new corporate campus on roomy, sprawling suburban greens. After completing their campus, they extended their rehab efforts outward in the form of no-interest loans, unending family assistance programs, and wasteful entrepreneurial incentives. Somehow they are still afloat, but you can bet the drain on their resources has been substantial.

N: *$22 Million Down The Drain*
Almost as much of a drain as, say, Yodaco?

22

RETIREMENT

H: *Eureka!*

A few months ago, somebody left a copy of an article on my desk. I set it aside, and didn't think about it again until one morning when I came in and spotted it on my chair. At the time, I figured that somehow the clipping had fallen off my desk or out of a drawer. Looking back I can see that fate was at work: I was destined to read that clipping.

When I finally sat down and read the words, I was cut to my very core. The article spoke to me, as if it had been written just for me. That night I sat in my spa with a gin and tonic and had the first heart-to-heart talk with myself I've had in a long time.

What did the watershed article say? It eloquently told the story of an obsessive and hard-driving CEO, legendary for his 100-hour workweeks, who had suddenly announced his retirement. Nothing too strange there. What hit me like Millicent's hind leg was the reason *why.* This contemporary of mine had realized that it was "high time" he spent more quality time with his possessions.

"I took a long, hard look at my Mercedes CL500 Coupe and

realized it wasn't getting any newer," the article quoted the CEO, a husband and father of three, as saying. "After spending most of my life putting my career before everything else, it suddenly dawned on me that I was missing out on what really matters: My luxury goods."

This man had put into words a feeling that had been gnawing away at me deep inside for too many years. All of my hard work had brought me the lifestyle to which I aspired, but I had not taken full advantage. No wonder I'd felt like there was something missing. Suddenly, I knew! I already had what I'd wanted all along—I just wasn't enjoying it to the fullest!

At that moment I made the decision to formally retire. It was time to turn out the light, lock the door, throw away the key (well, maybe I'd keep the key), and sail off to Bermuda. My generation had lived a life of purpose: Winning wars and building this country. Now what? We didn't need anything more. Our race was run, and run well. Retirement was the finish line.

N: *Shell Game*

I can't believe Hub fell for that *Onion* article!

Actually, there was another reason Hub suddenly decided to retire. It had to do with the SEC's curiosity over financial losses quietly shifted to one of Ablebright Manufacturing's so-called partnerships: Yodaco. No wonder Ablebright's bottom line always looked so healthy!

H: *I'm Clean!*

I don't know a thing about it. The CFO swore it was an honest mistake. The Feds never proved any intent—he'll walk away a free man. So, pin that tale on some other donkey.

N: *Protected Species*

What do undersized fish and indicted executives have in common? They're both catch-and-release.

H: *Party Time*

The retirement party unfolded as I have described in a previous chapter, with one significant postscript. What I hadn't expected was the visit from Nicholas, who showed up in a suit (he also sported a goatee and an earring, but I was touched nonetheless) and presented me with a gift.

"Best wishes," he said.

I carefully opened the small box, having no idea what to expect. An engraved Cartier watch perhaps? I'd heard his studio venture was picking up steam. I removed the lid.

Inside was a photo of Nicholas and me grinning and shaking hands on a golf course somewhere. Beneath it was my old four-leaf clover ball marker.

"I managed to find it before we left," he said.

I stared at the gift and felt my face flush.

"I know it's not much," he added.

He was certainly right about that!

"Thanks," I muttered.

It's a damn good thing today's retirees don't have to rely on the younger generation to take care of them in their retirement. The young would jam them into some cheap apartment, fill their cupboards with generic oatmeal, and spend all of their money.

N: *A Revelation*

There were several reasons I ditched the corporate world, but there's one I just figured out. At the time I left I knew I didn't want all of the hassles that come with being part of top management. The money's good—no doubt—but the stress just isn't worth it.

Now, I realize you don't have to "put out" as much as I thought. I was worried that I'd have to be this super-competent, super-caring hero performing at a really high level. Not true! While there are plenty of talented executives, there are just as many who slum their way through and collect their big paydays anyway. They rise to their "level of incompetence," but they hardly ever get fired. Even when they do, they still have "experience," and there are plenty of other places to go where no one knows them.

That said, I'm definitely sticking with the studio thing. I'm starting to make some decent money and have added two partners. The main thing is, I am totally amped up about going in to "work" every day and being creative as I lay down my own tracks or help other artists.

Maybe someday I'll have my own corporation. I'm not sure yet how I'd run it, but I know how I *wouldn't* run it. I guess that's the thing about coming ashore later—you see some things. . . .